Course	Integrated Perspectives
Course Number	**GBA 398**
Professor	Andrew Gold
	Saint Leo University
	School of Business

http://create.mheducation.com

ISBN-10: 1308406738   ISBN-13: 9781308406732

Contents

Credits

Guide to Case Analysis

I keep six honest serving men
(They taught me all I knew);
Their names are What and Why and When;
And How and Where and Who.

Rudyard Kipling

n most courses in strategic management, students use cases about actual companies to practice strategic analysis and to gain some experience in the tasks of crafting and implementing strategy. A case sets forth, in a factual manner, the events and organizational circumstances surrounding a particular managerial situation. It puts readers at the scene of the action and familiarizes them with all the relevant circumstances. A case on strategic management can concern a whole industry, a single organization, or some part of an organization; the organization involved can be either profit seeking or not-for-profit. The essence of the student's role in case analysis is to *diagnose* and *size up* the situation described in the case and then to *recommend* appropriate action steps.

WHY USE CASES TO PRACTICE STRATEGIC MANAGEMENT?

> A student of business with tact
> Absorbed many answers he lacked.
> But acquiring a job,
> He said with a sob,
> "How does one fit answer to fact?"

The foregoing limerick was used some years ago by Professor Charles Gragg to characterize the plight of business students who had no exposure to cases.[1] The facts are that the mere act of listening to lectures and sound advice about managing does little for anyone's management skills and that the accumulated managerial wisdom cannot effectively be passed on by lectures and assigned readings alone. If anything had been learned about the practice of management, it is that a storehouse of ready-made textbook answers does not exist. Each managerial situation has unique aspects, requiring its own diagnosis, judgment, and tailor-made actions. Cases provide would-be managers with a valuable way to practice wrestling with the actual problems of actual managers in actual companies.

The case approach to strategic analysis is, first and foremost, an exercise in learning by doing. Because cases provide you with detailed information about conditions and problems of different industries and companies, your task of analyzing company after company and situation after situation has the twin benefit of boosting your analytical skills and exposing you to the ways companies and managers actually do things. Most college students have limited managerial backgrounds and only fragmented knowledge about companies and real-life strategic situations. Cases help substitute for on-the-job experience by (1) giving you broader exposure to a variety of industries, organizations, and strategic problems; (2) forcing you to assume a managerial role (as opposed to that of just an onlooker); (3) providing a test of how to apply the tools and techniques of strategic management; and (4) asking you to come up with pragmatic managerial action plans to deal with the issues at hand.

Objectives of Case Analysis

Using cases to learn about the practice of strategic management is a powerful way for you to accomplish five things:[2]

1. *Increase your understanding of what managers should and should not do in guiding a business to success.*

2. *Build your skills in sizing up company resource strengths and weaknesses and in conducting strategic analysis in a variety of industries and competitive situations.*

3. *Get valuable practice in identifying strategic issues that need to be addressed, evaluating strategic alternatives, and formulating workable plans of action.*

4. *Enhance your sense of business judgment, as opposed to uncritically accepting the authoritative crutch of the professor or "back-of-the-book" answers.*

5. *Gaining in-depth exposure to different industries and companies, thereby acquiring something close to actual business experience.*

If you understand that these are the objectives of case analysis, you are less likely to be consumed with curiosity about "the answer to the case." Students who have grown comfortable with and accustomed to textbook statements of fact and definitive lecture notes are often frustrated when discussions about a case do not produce concrete answers. Usually, case discussions produce good arguments for more than one course of action. Differences of opinion nearly always exist. Thus, should a class discussion conclude without a strong, unambiguous consensus on what to do, don't grumble too much when you are not told what the answer is or what the company actually did. Just remember that in the business world answers don't come in conclusive black-and-white terms. There are nearly always several feasible courses of action and approaches, each of which may work out satisfactorily. Moreover, in the business world, when one elects a particular course of action, there is no peeking at the back of a book to see if you have chosen the best thing to do and no one to turn to for a probably correct answer. The best test of whether management action is "right" or "wrong" is *results*. If the results of an action turn out to be "good," the decision to take it may be presumed "right." If not, then the action chosen was "wrong" in the sense that it didn't work out

Hence, the important thing for you to understand about analyzing cases is that the managerial exercise of identifying, diagnosing, and recommending is aimed at building your skills of business judgment. Discovering what the company actually did is no more than frosting on the cake—the actions that company managers actually took may or may not be "right" or best (unless there is accompanying evidence that the results of their actions were highly positive.

The point is this: *The purpose of giving you a case assignment is not to cause you to run to the library or surf the Internet to discover what the company actually did but, rather, to enhance your skills in sizing up situations and developing your managerial judgment about what needs to be done and how to do it.* The aim of case analysis is for you to become actively engaged in diagnosing the business issues and managerial problems posed in the case, to propose workable solutions, and to explain and defend your assessments—this is how cases provide you with meaningful practice at being a manager.

Preparing a Case for Class Discussion

If this is your first experience with the case method, you may have to reorient your study habits. Unlike lecture courses where you can get by without preparing intensively for each class and where you have latitude to work assigned readings and reviews of lecture notes into your schedule, a case assignment requires conscientious preparation before class. You will not get much out of hearing the class discuss a case you haven't read, and you certainly won't be able to contribute anything yourself to the discussion. What you have got to do to get ready for class discussion of a case is to study the case, reflect carefully on the situation presented, and develop some reasoned thoughts. Your goal in preparing the case should be to end up with what you think is a sound, well-supported analysis of the situation and a sound, defensible set of recommendations about which managerial actions need to be taken.

To prepare a case for class discussion, we suggest the following approach:

1. *Skim the case rather quickly to get an overview of the situation it presents.* This quick overview should give you the general flavor of the situation and indicate the kinds of issues and problems that you will need to wrestle with. If your instructor has provided you with study questions for the case, now is the time to read them carefully.

2. *Read the case thoroughly to digest the facts and circumstances.* On this reading, try to gain full command of the situation presented in the case. Begin to develop some tentative answers to the study questions your instructor has provided. If your instructor has elected not to give you assignment questions, then start forming your own picture of the overall situation being described.

3. *Carefully review all the information presented in the exhibits.* Often, there is an important story in the numbers contained in the exhibits. Expect the information in the case exhibits to be crucial enough to materially affect your diagnosis of the situation.

4. *Decide what the strategic issues are.* Until you have identified the strategic issues and problems in the case, you don't know what to analyze, which tools and analytical techniques are called for, or otherwise how to proceed. At times the strategic issues are clear—either being stated in the case or else obvious from reading the case. At other times you will have to dig them out from all the information given; if so, the study questions will guide you.

5. *Start your analysis of the issues with some number crunching.* A big majority of strategy cases call for some kind of number crunching—calculating assorted financial ratios to check out the company's financial condition and recent performance, calculating growth rates of sales or profits or unit volume, checking out profit margins and the makeup of the cost structure, and understanding whatever revenue-cost-profit relationships are present. See Table 1 for a summary of key financial ratios, how they are calculated, and what they show.

6. *Apply the concepts and techniques of strategic analysis you have been studying.* Strategic analysis is not just a collection of opinions; rather, it entails applying the concepts and analytical tools described in Chapters 1 through 13 to cut beneath the surface and produce sharp insight and understanding. Every case assigned is strategy related and presents you with an opportunity to usefully apply what you have learned. Your instructor is looking for you to demonstrate that you know how and when to use the material presented in the text chapters.

7. *Check out conflicting opinions and make some judgments about the validity of all the data and*

CA4   **STRATEGY:** Core Concepts and Analytical Approaches

TABLE 1   Key Financial Ratios: How to Calculate Them and What They Mean

Ratio	How Calculated	What It Shows
Profitability Ratios		
1. Gross profit margin	$$\frac{\text{Sales} - \text{Cost of goods sold}}{\text{Sales}}$$	Shows the percentage of revenues available to cover operating expenses and yield a profit. Higher is better and the trend should be upward.
2. Operating profit margin (or return on sales)	$$\frac{\text{Sales} - \text{Operating expenses}}{\text{Sales}}$$ or $$\frac{\text{Operating income}}{\text{Sales}}$$	Shows the profitability of current operations without regard to interest charges and income taxes. Higher is better and the trend should be upward.
3. Net profit margin (or net return on sales)	$$\frac{\text{Profits after taxes}}{\text{Sales}}$$	Shows after-tax profits per dollar of sales. Higher is better and the trend should be upward.
4. Total return on assets	$$\frac{\text{Profits after taxes} + \text{Interest}}{\text{Total assets}}$$	A measure of the return on total monetary investment in the enterprise. Interest is added to after-tax profits to form the numerator since total assets are financed by creditors as well as by stockholders. Higher is better and the trend should be upward.
5. Net return on total assets (ROA)	$$\frac{\text{Profits after taxes}}{\text{Total assets}}$$	A measure of the return earned by stockholders on the firm's total assets. Higher is better, and the trend should be upward.
6. Return on stockholder's equity (ROE)	$$\frac{\text{Profits after taxes}}{\text{Total stockholders' equity}}$$	Shows the return stockholders are earning on their capital investment in the enterprise. A return in the 12–15% range is "average," and the trend should be upward.
7. Return on invested capital (ROIC)— sometimes referred to as return on capital employed (ROCE)	$$\frac{\text{Profits after taxes}}{\text{Long-term debt} + \text{Total stockholders' equity}}$$	A measure of the return shareholders are earning on the long-term monetary capital invested in the enterprise. A higher return reflects greater bottom-line effectiveness in the use of long-term capital, and the trend should be upward.
8. Earnings per share (EPS)	$$\frac{\text{Profits after taxes}}{\text{Number of shares of common stock outstanding}}$$	Shows the earnings for each share of common stock outstanding. The trend should be upward, and the bigger the annual percentage gains, the better.
Liquidity Ratios		
1. Current ratio	$$\frac{\text{Current assets}}{\text{Current liabilities}}$$	Shows a firm's ability to pay current liabilities using assets that can be converted to cash in the near term. Ratio should definitely be higher than 1.0; ratios of 2 or higher are better still.
2. Working capital	$\text{Current assets} - \text{Current liabilities}$	Bigger amounts are better because the company has more internal funds available to (1) pay its current liabilities on a timely basis and (2) finance inventory expansion, additional accounts receivable, and a larger base of operations without resorting to borrowing or raising more equity capital.
Leverage Ratios		
1. Total debt-to-assets ratio	$$\frac{\text{Total debt}}{\text{Total assets}}$$	Measures the extent to which borrowed funds have been used to finance the firm's operations. Low fractions or ratios are better—high fractions indicate overuse of debt and greater risk of bankruptcy.
2. Long-term debt-to-capital ratio	$$\frac{\text{Long-term debt}}{\text{Long-term debt} + \text{Total stockholders' equity}}$$	An important measure of creditworthiness and balance sheet strength. Indicates the percentage of capital investment which has been financed by creditors and bondholders. Fractions or ratios below .25 or 25% are usually quite satisfactory since monies invested

(Continued)

A Guide to Case Analysis   **CA5**

TABLE 1   (*Continued*)

Leverage Ratios (*Continued*)

		by stockholders account for 75% or more of the company's total capital. The lower the ratio, the greater the capacity to borrow additional funds. Debt-to capital ratios above 50% and certainly above 75% indicate a heavy and perhaps excessive reliance on debt, lower creditworthiness, and weak balance sheet strength.
3. Debt-to-equity ratio	$\dfrac{\text{Total debt}}{\text{Total stockholders' equity}}$	Should usually be less than 1.0. High ratios (especially above 1.0) signal excessive debt, lower creditworthiness, and weaker balance sheet strength.
4. Long-term debt-to-equity ratio	$\dfrac{\text{Long-term debt}}{\text{Total stockholders' equity}}$	Shows the balance between debt and equity in the firm's *long-term* capital structure. Low ratios indicate greater capacity to borrow additional funds if needed.
4. Times-interest-earned (or coverage) ratio	$\dfrac{\text{Operating income}}{\text{Interest expenses}}$	Measures the ability to pay annual interest charges. Lenders usually insist on a minimum ratio of 2.0, but ratios above 3.0 signal better creditworthiness.

Activity Ratios

1. Days of inventory	$\dfrac{\text{Inventory}}{\text{Cost of goods sold} \div 365}$	Measures inventory management efficiency. Fewer days of inventory are usually better.
2. Inventory turnover	$\dfrac{\text{Cost of goods sold}}{\text{Inventory}}$	Measures the number of inventory turns per year. Higher is better.
3. Average collection period	$\dfrac{\text{Accounts receivable}}{\text{Total sales revenues} \div 365}$ or $\dfrac{\text{Accounts receivable}}{\text{Average daily sales}}$	Indicates the average length of time the firm must wait after making a sale to receive cash payment. A shorter collection time is better.

Other Important Measures of Financial Performance

1. Dividend yield on common stock	$\dfrac{\text{Annual dividends per share}}{\text{Current market price per share}}$	A measure of the return that shareholders receive in the form of dividends. A "typical" dividend yield is 2–3%. The dividend yield for fast-growth companies is often below 1% (maybe even 0); the dividend yield for slow-growth companies can run 4–5%.
2. Price-earnings ratio	$\dfrac{\text{Current market price per share}}{\text{Earnings per share}}$	P-e ratios above 20 indicate strong investor confidence in a firm's outlook and earnings growth; firms whose future earnings are at risk or likely to grow slowly typically have ratios below 12.
3. Dividend payout ratio	$\dfrac{\text{Annual dividends per share}}{\text{Earnings per share}}$	Indicates the percentage of after-tax profits paid cut as dividends.
4. Internal cash flow	After tax profits + Depreciation	A quick and rough estimate of the c business is generating after payment of operating expenses, interest, and taxes. Such amounts can be used for dividend payments or funding capital expenditures.
5. Free cash flow	After tax profits + Depreciation − Capital expenditures − Dividends	A quick and rough estimate of the cash a company's business is generating after payment of operating expenses, interest, taxes, dividends, and desirable reinvestments in the business. The larger a company's free cash flow, the greater is its ability to internally fund new strategic initiatives, repay debt, make new acquisitions, repurchase shares of stock, or increase dividend payments.

information provided. Many times cases report views and contradictory opinions (after all, people don't always agree on things, and different people see the same things in different ways). Forcing you to evaluate the data and information presented in the case helps you develop your powers of inference and judgment. Asking you to resolve conflicting information "comes with the territory" because a great many managerial situations entail opposing points of view, conflicting trends, and sketchy information.

8. *Support your diagnosis and opinions with reasons and evidence.* The most important things to prepare for are your answers to the question "Why?" For instance, if after studying the case you are of the opinion that the company's managers are doing a poor job, then it is your answer to "Why?" that establishes just how good your analysis of the situation is. If your instructor has provided you with specific study questions for the case, by all means prepare answers that include all the reasons and number-crunching evidence you can muster to support your diagnosis. If you are using study questions provided by the instructor, *generate at least two pages of notes!*

9. *Develop an appropriate action plan and set of recommendations.* Diagnosis divorced from corrective action is sterile. The test of a manager is always to convert sound analysis into sound actions—actions that will produce the desired results. Hence, the final and most telling step in preparing a case is to develop an action agenda for management that lays out a set of specific recommendations on what to do. Bear in mind that proposing realistic, workable solutions is far preferable to casually tossing out off-the-top-of-your-head suggestions. Be prepared to argue why your recommendations are more attractive than other courses of action that are open.

As long as you are conscientious in preparing your analysis and recommendations, and have ample reasons, evidence, and arguments to support your views, you shouldn't fret unduly about whether what you've prepared is "the right answer" to the case. In case analysis, there is rarely just one right approach or set of recommendations. Managing companies and crafting and executing strategies are not such exact sciences that there exists a single provably correct analysis and action plan for each strategic situation. Of course, some analyses and action plans are better than others; but, in truth, there's nearly always more than one good way to analyze a situation and more than one good plan of action.

Participating in Class Discussion of a Case

Classroom discussions of cases are sharply different from attending a lecture class. In a case class, students do most of the talking. The instructor's role is to solicit student participation, keep the discussion on track, ask "Why?" often, offer alternative views, play the devil's advocate (if no students jump in to offer opposing views), and otherwise lead the discussion. The students in the class carry the burden for analyzing the situation and for being prepared to present and defend their diagnoses and recommendations. Expect a classroom environment, therefore, that calls for your size-up of the situation, your analysis, what actions you would take, and why you would take them. Do not be dismayed if, as the class discussion unfolds, some insightful things are said by your fellow classmates that you did not think of. It is normal for views and analyses to differ and for the comments of others in the class to expand your own thinking about the case. As the old adage goes, "Two heads are better than one." So it is to be expected that the class as a whole will do a more penetrating and searching job of case analysis than will any one person working alone. This is the power of group effort, and its virtues are that it will help you see more analytical applications, let you test your analyses and judgments against those of your peers, and force you to wrestle with differences of opinion and approaches.

To orient you to the classroom environment on the days a case discussion is scheduled, we compiled the following list of things to expect

1. Expect the instructor to assume the role of extensive questioner and listener.

2. Expect students to do most of the talking. The case method enlists a maximum of individual participation in class discussion. It is not enough to be present as a silent observer; if every student took this approach, there would be no discussion. (Thus, expect a portion of your grade to be based on your participation in case discussions.)

3. Be prepared for the instructor to probe for reasons and supporting analysis.

4. Expect and tolerate challenges to the views expressed. All students have to be willing to submit their conclusions for scrutiny and rebuttal. Each student needs to learn to state his or her views

without fear of disapproval and to overcome the hesitation of speaking out. Learning respect for the views and approaches of others is an integral part of case analysis exercises. But there are times when it is OK to swim against the tide of majority opinion. In the practice of management, there is always room for originality and unorthodox approaches. So while discussion of a case is a group process, there is no compulsion for you or anyone else to cave in and conform to group opinions and group consensus.

5. Don't be surprised if you change your mind about some things as the discussion unfolds. Be alert to how these changes affect your analysis and recommendations (in the event you get called on).

6. Expect to learn a lot in class as the discussion of a case progresses; furthermore, you will find that the cases build on one another—what you learn in one case helps prepare you for the next case discussion.

There are several things you can do on your own to be good and look good as a participant in class discussions:

Although you should do your own independent work and independent thinking, don't hesitate before (and after) class to discuss the case with other students. In real life, managers often discuss the company's problems and situation with other people to refine their own thinking.

- In participating in the discussion, make a conscious effort to contribute, rather than just talk. There is a big difference between saying something that builds the discussion and offering a long-winded, off-the-cuff remark that leaves the class wondering what the point was.

- Avoid the use of "I think," "I believe," and "I feel"; instead, say, "My analysis shows —" and "The company should do _____ because _____." Always give supporting reasons and evidence for your views; then your instructor won't have to ask you "Why?" every time you make a comment.

- In making your points, assume that everyone has read the case and knows what it says. Avoid reciting and rehashing information in the case—instead, use the data and information to explain your assessment of the situation and to support your position.

- Bring the printouts of the work you've done on Case-Tutor or the notes you've prepared (usually two or three pages' worth) to class and rely on them

extensively when you speak. There's no way you can remember everything off the top of your head—especially the results of your number crunching. To reel off the numbers or to present all five reasons why, instead of one, you will need good notes. When you have prepared thoughtful answers to the study questions and use them as the basis for your comments, *everybody* in the room will know you are well prepared, and your contribution to the case discussion will stand out.

Preparing a Written Case Analysis

Preparing a written case analysis is much like preparing a case for class discussion, except that your analysis must be more complete and put in report form. Unfortunately, though, there is no ironclad procedure for doing a written case analysis. All we can offer are some general guidelines and words of wisdom—this is because company situations and management problems are so diverse that no one mechanical way to approach a written case assignment always works.

Your instructor may assign you a specific topic around which to prepare your written report. Or, alternatively, you may be asked to do a comprehensive written case analysis, where the expectation is that you will (1) *identify* all the pertinent issues that management needs to address, (2) perform whatever *analysis* and *evaluation* is appropriate, and (3) propose an *action plan* and *set of recommendations* addressing the issues you have identified. In going through the exercise of identify, evaluate, and recommend, keep the following pointers in mind.[3]

Identification   It is essential early on in your paper that you provide a sharply focused diagnosis of strategic issues and key problems and that you demonstrate a good grasp of the company's present situation. Make sure you can identify the firm's strategy (use the concepts and tools in Chapters 1–8 as diagnostic aids) and that you can pinpoint whatever strategy implementation issues may exist (again, consult the material in Chapters 9–11 for diagnostic help). Consult the key points we have provided at the end of each chapter for further diagnostic suggestions. Consider beginning your paper with an overview of the company's situation, its strategy, and the significant problems and issues that confront management. State problems/issues as clearly and precisely as you can. Unless it is necessary to do so for emphasis, avoid recounting facts and history about the company (assume your professor has read the case and is familiar with the organization).

Analysis and Evaluation This is usually the hardest part of the report. Analysis is hard work! Check out the firm's financial ratios, its profit margins and rates of return, and its capital structure, and decide how strong the firm is financially. Table 1 contains a summary of various financial ratios and how they are calculated. Use it to assist in your financial diagnosis. Similarly, look at marketing, production, managerial competence, and other factors underlying the organization's strategic successes and failures. Decide whether the firm has valuable resource strengths and competencies and, if so, whether it is capitalizing on them.

Check to see if the firm's strategy is producing satisfactory results and determine the reasons why or why not. Probe the nature and strength of the competitive forces confronting the company. Decide whether and why the firm's competitive position is getting stronger or weaker. Use the tools and concepts you have learned about to perform whatever analysis and evaluation is appropriate. Work through the case preparation exercise on Case-Tutor if one is available for the case you've been assigned.

In writing your analysis and evaluation, bear in mind four things:

1. You are obliged to offer analysis and evidence to back up your conclusions. Do not rely on unsupported opinions, over-generalizations, and platitudes as a substitute for tight, logical argument backed up with facts and figures.

2. If your analysis involves some important quantitative calculations, use tables and charts to present the calculations clearly and efficiently. Don't just tack the exhibits on at the end of your report and let the reader figure out what they mean and why they were included. Instead, in the body of your report cite some of the key numbers, highlight the conclusions to be drawn from the exhibits, and refer the reader to your charts and exhibits for more details.

3. Demonstrate that you have command of the strategic concepts and analytical tools to which you have been exposed. Use them in your report.

4. Your interpretation of the evidence should be reasonable and objective. Be wary of preparing a one-sided argument that omits all aspects not favorable to your conclusions. Likewise, try not to exaggerate or overdramatize. Endeavor to inject balance into your analysis and to avoid emotional rhetoric. Strike phrases such as "I think," "I feel," and "I believe" when you edit your first draft and write in "My analysis shows," instead.

Recommendations The final section of the written case analysis should consist of a set of definite recommendations and a plan of action. Your set of recommendations should address all of the problems/issues you identified and analyzed. If the recommendations come as a surprise or do not follow logically from the analysis, the effect is to weaken greatly your suggestions of what to do. Obviously, your recommendations for actions should offer a reasonable prospect of success. High-risk, bet-the-company recommendations should be made with caution. State how your recommendations will solve the problems you identified. Be sure the company is financially able to carry out what you recommend; also check to see if your recommendations are workable in terms of acceptance by the persons involved, the organization's competence to implement them, and prevailing market and environmental constraints. Try not to hedge or weasel on the actions you believe should be taken.

By all means state your recommendations in sufficient detail to be meaningful—get down to some definite nitty-gritty specifics. Avoid such unhelpful statements as "the organization should do more planning" or "the company should be more aggressive in marketing its product." For instance, if you determine that "the firm should improve its market position," then you need to set forth exactly how you think this should be done. Offer a definite agenda for action, stipulating a timetable and sequence for initiating actions, indicating priorities, and suggesting who should be responsible for doing what.

In proposing an action plan, remember there is a great deal of difference between, on the one hand, being responsible for a decision that may be costly if it proves in error and, on the other hand, casually suggesting courses of action that might be taken when you do not have to bear the responsibility for any of the consequences.

A good rule to follow in making your recommendations is: *Avoid recommending anything you would not yourself be willing to do if you were in management's shoes.* The importance of learning to develop good managerial judgment is indicated by the fact that, even though the same information and operating data may be available to every manager or executive in an organization, the quality of the judgments about what the information means and which actions need to be taken does vary from person to person.[4]

It goes without saying that your report should be well organized and well written. Great ideas amount to little unless others can be convinced of their merit—this takes tight logic, the presentation of convincing evidence, and persuasively written arguments.

Preparing an Oral Presentation

During the course of your business career it is very likely that you will be called upon to prepare and give a number of oral presentations. For this reason, it is common in courses of this nature to assign cases for oral presentation to the whole class. Such assignments give you an opportunity to hone your presentation skills.

The preparation of an oral presentation has much in common with that of a written case analysis. Both require identification of the strategic issues and problems confronting the company, analysis of industry conditions and the company's situation, and the development of a thorough, well-thought out action plan. The substance of your analysis and quality of your recommendations in an oral presentation should be no different than in a written report. As with a written assignment, you'll need to demonstrate command of the relevant strategic concepts and tools of analysis and your recommendations should contain sufficient detail to provide clear direction for management. The main difference between an oral presentation and a written case is in the delivery format. Oral presentations rely principally on verbalizing your diagnosis, analysis, and recommendations and visually enhancing and supporting your oral discussion with colorful, snappy slides (usually created on Microsoft's Power-Point software).

Typically, oral presentations involve group assignments. Your instructor will provide the details of the assignment—how work should be delegated among the group members and how the presentation should be conducted. Some instructors prefer that presentations begin with issue identification, followed by analysis of the industry and company situation analysis, and conclude with a recommended action plan to improve company performance. Other instructors prefer that the presenters assume that the class has a good understanding of the external industry environment and the company's competitive position and expect the presentation to be strongly focused on the group's recommended action plan and supporting analysis and arguments. The latter approach requires cutting straight to the heart of the case and supporting each recommendation with detailed analysis and persuasive reasoning. Still other instructors may give

you the latitude to structure your presentation however you and your group members see fit.

Regardless of the style preferred by your instructor, you should take great care in preparing for the presentation. A good set of slides with good content and good visual appeal is essential to a first-rate presentation. Take some care to choose a nice slide design, font size and style, and color scheme. We suggest including slides covering each of the following areas:

- An opening slide covering the "title" of the presentation and names of the presenters.
- A slide showing an outline of the presentation (perhaps with presenters' names by each topic).
- One or more slides showing the key problems and strategic issues that management needs to address.
- A series of slides covering your analysis of the company's situation.
- A series of slides containing your recommendations and the supporting arguments and reasoning for each recommendation—one slide for each recommendation and the associated reasoning will give it a lot of merit.

You and your team members should carefully plan and rehearse your slide show to maximize impact and minimize distractions. The slide show should include all of the pizzazz necessary to garner the attention of the audience, but not so much that it distracts from the content of what group members are saying to the class. You should remember that the role of slides is to help you communicate your points to the audience. Too many graphics, images, colors, and transitions may divert the audience's attention from what is being said or disrupt the flow of the presentation. Keep in mind that visually dazzling slides rarely hide a shallow or superficial or otherwise flawed case analysis from a perceptive audience. Most instructors will tell you that first-rate slides will definitely enhance a well-delivered presentation, but that impressive visual aids, if accompanied by weak analysis and poor oral delivery, still add up to a substandard presentation.

Researching Companies and Industries via the Internet and Online Data Services

Very likely, there will be occasions when you need to get additional information about some of the assignee cases, perhaps because your instructor has asked you to do further research on the industry or company or because you are simply curious about what has happened to the company since the case was written. These days, it is relatively easy to run down recent industry developments and to find out whether a company's strategic and financial situation has improved, deteriorated, or changed little since the conclusion of the case. The amount of information about companies and industries available on the Internet and through online data services is formidable and expanding rapidly.

It is a fairly simple matter to go to company websites, click on the investor information offerings and press release files, and get quickly to useful information. Most company websites allow you to view or print the company's quarterly and annual reports, its 10K and 10Q filings with the Securities and Exchange Commission, and various company press releases of interest. Frequently, a company's website will also provide information about its mission and vision statements, values statements, codes of ethics, and strategy information, as well as charts of the company's stock price. The company's recent press releases typically contain reliable information about what of interest has been going on—new product introductions, recent alliances and partnership agreements, recent acquisitions, summaries of the latest financial results, tidbits about the company's strategy, guidance about future revenues and earnings, and other late-breaking company developments. Some company web pages also include links to the home pages of industry trade associations where you can find information about industry size, growth, recent industry news, statistical trends, and future outlook. Thus, an early step in researching a company on the Internet is always to go to its website and see what's available.

Online Data Services

Lexis-Nexis, Bloomberg Financial News Services, and other online subscription services available in many university libraries provide access to a wide array of business reference material. For example, the web-based Lexis-Nexis Academic Universe contains business news articles from general news sources, business publications, and industry trade publications. Broadcast transcripts from financial news programs are also available through Lexis-Nexis, as are full-text 10-Ks, 10-Qs, annual reports, and company profiles for more than 11,000 U.S. and international companies. Your business librarian should be able to direct you to the resources available through your library that will aid you in your research.

Public and Subscription Websites with Good Information

Plainly, you can use a search engine such as Google or Yahoo! or MSN to find the latest news on a company or articles written by reporters that have appeared in the business media. These can be very valuable in running down information about recent company developments. However, keep in mind that the information retrieved by a search engine is "unfiltered" and may include sources that are not reliable or that contain inaccurate or misleading information. Be wary of information provided by authors who are unaffiliated with reputable organizations or publications and articles that were published in off-beat sources or on websites with an agenda. Be especially careful in relying on the accuracy of information you find posted on various bulletin boards. Articles covering a company or issue should be copyrighted or published by a reputable source. If you are turning in a paper containing information gathered from the Internet, you should cite your sources (providing the Internet address and date visited); it is also wise to print web pages for your research file (some web pages are updated frequently).

The Wall Street Journal, Bloomberg Businessweek, Forbes, Barron's, and *Fortune* are all good sources of articles on companies. The online edition of *The Wall Street Journal* contains the same information that is available daily in its print version of the paper, but the WSJ website also maintains a searchable database of all *The Wall Street Journal* articles published during the past few years. *Fortune* and *Bloomberg Businessweek* also make the content of the most current issue available online to subscribers as well as provide archives sections that allow you to search for articles published during the past few years that may be related to a particular keyword.

The following publications and websites are particularly good sources of company and industry information:

Securities and Exchange Commission EDGAR database (contains company 10-Ks, 10-Qs, etc.)
   http://www.sec.gov/edgar/searchedgar/companysearch
Google Finance
   http://finance.google.com
CNN Money
   http://money.cnn.com
Hoover's Online
   http://hoovers.com
The Wall Street Journal Interactive Edition
   www.wsj.com
Bloomberg Businessweek
   www.businessweek.com and www.bloomberg.com

Fortune
www.fortune.com
MSN Money Central
http://moneycentral.msn.com
Yahoo! Finance
http://finance.yahoo.com/

Some of these Internet sources require subscriptions in order to access their entire databases.

You should/always explore the investor relations section of every public company's website. In today's world, these websites typically have a wealth of information concerning a company's mission, core values, performance targets, strategy, recent financial performance, and latest developments (as described in company press releases).

Learning Comes Quickly With a modest investment of time, you will learn how to use Internet sources and search engines to run down information on companies and industries quickly and efficiently. And it is a skill that will serve you well into the future. Once you become familiar with the data available at the different websites mentioned above and learn how to use a search engine, you will know where to go to look for the particular information that you want. Search engines nearly always turn up too many information sources that match your request rather than too few. The trick is to learn to zero in on those most relevant to what you are looking for. Like most things, once you get a little experience under your belt on how to do company and industry research on the Internet, you will find that you can readily find the information you need.

The Ten Commandments of Case Analysis

As a way of summarizing our suggestions about how to approach the task of case analysis, we have we like to call "The Ten Commandments of Case Analysis." They are shown in Table 2. If you observe all or even most of these commandments faithfully as you prepare a case either for class discussion or for a written report, your chances of doing a good job on the assigned cases will be much improved. Hang in there, give it your best shot, and have some fun exploring what the real world of strategic management is all about.

TABLE 2   **The Ten Commandments of Case Analysis**

To be observed in written reports and oral presentations, and while participating in class discussions.

1. Go through the case twice, once for a quick overview and once to gain full command of the facts. Then take care to explore the information in every one of the case exhibits.

2. Make a complete list of the problems and issues that the company's management needs to address.

3. Be thorough in your analysis of the company's situation (make a minimum of one to two pages of notes detailing your diagnosis).

4. Look for opportunities to apply the concepts and analytical tools in the text chapters—all of the cases in the book have very definite ties to the material in one or more of the text chapters!!!!

5. Do enough number crunching to discover the story told by the data presented in the case. (To help you comply with this commandment, consult Table 1 in this section to guide your probing of a company's financial condition and financial performance.)

6. Support any and all off-the-cuff opinions with well-reasoned arguments and numerical evidence. Don't stop until you can purge "I think" and "I feel" from your assessment and, instead, are able to rely completely on "My analysis shows."

7. Prioritize your recommendations and make sure they can be carried out in an acceptable time frame with the available resources.

8. Support each recommendation with persuasive argument and reasons as to why it makes sense and should result in improved company performance.

9. Review your recommended action plan to see if it addresses all of the problems and issues you identified. Any set of recommendations that does not address all of the issues and problems you identified is incomplete and insufficient.

10. Avoid recommending any course of action that could have disastrous consequences if it doesn't work out as planned. Therefore be as alert to the downside risks of your recommendations as you are to their upside potential and appeal.

CA12   **STRATEGY:** Core Concepts and Analytical Approaches

ENDNOTES

[1] Charles I. Gragg, "Because Wisdom Can't Be Told," in *The Case Method at the Harvard Business School,* ed. M. P. McNair (New York: McGraw-Hill, 1954), p. 11.

[2] Ibid., pp. 12–14; and D. R. Schoen and Philip A. Sprague, "What Is the Case Method?" in *The Case Method at the Harvard Business School,* ed. M. P. McNair, pp. 78–79.

[3] For some additional ideas and viewpoints, you may wish to consult Thomas J. Raymond, "Written Analysis of Cases," in *The Case Method at the Harvard Business School,* ed. M. P. McNair, pp. 139–63. Raymond's article includes an actual case, a sample analysis of the case, and a sample of a student's written report on the case.

[4] Gragg, "Because Wisdom Can't Be Told," p. 10.

HARVARD | BUSINESS | SCHOOL

9-376-241
REV. APRIL 16, 2002

JOHN S. HAMMOND

Learning by the Case Method

The case method is not only the most relevant and practical way to learn managerial skills, it's exciting and fun. But, it can also be very confusing if you don't know much about it. This brief note is designed to remove the confusion by explaining how the case method works and then to suggest how you can get the most out of it.

Simply stated, the case method calls for discussion of *real-life situations* that business executives have faced. Casewriters, as good reporters, have written up these situations to present you with the information available to the executives involved. As you review their cases you will put yourself in the shoes of the managers, analyze the situation, decide what you would do, and come to class prepared to present and support your conclusions.

How Cases Help You Learn

Cases will help you sharpen your analytical skills, since you must produce quantitative and qualitative evidence to support your recommendations. In case discussions, instructors will challenge you and your fellow participants to defend your arguments and analyses. You will hone both your problem-solving and your ability to think and reason rigorously.

Because case studies cut across a range of organizations and situations, they provide you with an exposure far greater than you are likely to experience in your day-to-day routine. They also permit you to build knowledge in various management subjects by dealing selectively and intensively with problems in each field. You will quickly recognize that the problems you face as a manager are not unique to one organization or industry. From this you will develop a more professional sense of management.

In class discussions, participants bring to bear their expertise, experience, observations, analyses, and rules of thumb. What each class member brings to identifying the central problems in a case, analyzing them, and proposing solutions is as important as the content of the case itself. The lessons of experience are tested as different participants present and defend their analyses, each based on different experiences and attitudes gained by working in different jobs. Your classmates and you will differ significantly on what's important and how to deal with common problems, interdependencies, organizational needs, and the impact of decisions in one sector of an organization upon other sectors.

Professor John S. Hammond prepared this note building on earlier notes by professors E. Raymond Corey and Martin Marshall of the Harvard Business School.

Perhaps the most important benefit of using cases is that they help managers learn how to determine what the real problem[1] is and to ask the right questions. An able business leader once commented: "Ninety per cent of the task of a top manager is to ask useful questions. Answers are relatively easy to find, but asking good questions is the most critical skill." The *discussion questions* suggested for each case are just to help you focus on certain aspects of the case. In presenting them the faculty is not preempting your task of identifying the problems in the case. You still must ask yourself: "What *really* are the problems which this manager has to resolve?" Too often, in real-life situations managers manipulate facts and figures without the problems having been specifically defined.

A final benefit that the faculty seeks is to reinvigorate the sense of fun and excitement that comes with being a manager. You will sense once again that being a manager is a great challenge—intellectually, politically, and socially.

In short, the case method is really a focused form of learning by doing.

How to Prepare a Case

The use of the case method calls first for you, working individually, to carefully read and to think about each case (typically about two hours of preparation time for each case are provided in the schedule). No single way to prepare a case works for everyone. However, here are some general guidelines that you can adapt to create a method that works best for you.

1. *Read the first few paragraphs, then go through the case almost as fast as you can turn the pages,* asking yourself, "What, broadly, is the case about, and what types of information am I being given to analyze?" You will find that the text description at the beginning is almost always followed by a series of exhibits that contain added quantitative and qualitative information for your analysis.

2. *Read the case very carefully, underlining key facts and writing marginal notes as you go.* Then ask yourself: "What are the basic problems these managers have to resolve?" Try hard to put yourself in the position of the managers in the case. Make the managers' problems *your* problems.

3. *Note the key problems or issues* on a pad of paper. Then go through the case again.

4. *Sort out the relevant considerations for each problem area.*

5. *Do appropriate qualitative and quantitative analysis.*

6. *Develop a set of recommendations, supported by your analysis* of the case data.

Until now, your best results will come if you have worked by yourself. However, if you have time before class, it is useful to engage in informal discussions with some of your fellow participants about the cases. This can be done at social hours, meals, or planned get-togethers. In fact, some people like to form discussion groups to conduct such discussions. (Discussion groups are important enough to be mandatory scheduled activities in many executive programs.) The purpose of these discussions is

---

[1] See, for example, Hammond, Keeney and Raiffa, *Smart Choices, A Practical Guide to Making Better Decisions,* Harvard Business School Press, 1999, especially Chapter 2.

not to develop a consensus of a "group" position; it is to help members refine, adjust and amplify their own thinking.

To maximize the benefit to you of this group process it is extremely important not to skip or skimp on the individual preparation beforehand. If you take the easy way out and just familiarize yourself with the facts, saving all preparation to be done with your discussion group, you will deprive yourself of the opportunity to practice the very skills that you wanted to obtain when you enrolled.

What Happens in Class

In class, your instructor usually will let members discuss whatever aspects of the case they wish. The faculty's job is to facilitate the discussion, to pose questions, prod, draw out people's reasoning, play the devil's advocate and highlight issues. A healthy debate and discussion will ensue. You will benefit most if you participate actively in that debate. Sometimes faculty will present conceptual frameworks and invite you to use them to organize your thoughts to create new insights. Other times they'll generalize, summarize, or tell about relevant situations in other companies.

They'll try to keep the discussion on track and moving forward. To do this, they'll usually organize and document the on-going debate on the blackboard. While faculty may suggest the pros and cons of a particular action, only occasionally will they give their own views. Their job isn't to help the class reach a consensus; in fact, often the thought process will be far more important than the conclusions. Near the end, instructors will summarize the discussion and draw out the useful lessons and observations which are inherent in the case situation and which emerge from the case discussion.

A typical request at the end of a discussion is "What's the answer?" The case method of learning does not provide *the* answer. Rather, various participants in the discussion will have developed and supported *several* viable "answers".

Business is not, at least not yet, an exact science. There is no single, demonstrably right answer to a business problem. For the student or business person it cannot be a matter of peeking in the back of a book to see if he or she has arrived at the right solution. In every business situation, there is always a reasonable possibility that the best answer has not yet been found—even by teachers.[2]

Sometimes when the faculty knows the outcome of the case they'll share it with you at the end of the discussion. While it is fascinating to learn how things actually turned out, the outcome isn't the answer either. It is simply one more answer, which you may feel is better or worse than yours. What is important is that *you* know what you would do in that situation and, most importantly, *why*, and that your skill at arriving at such conclusions has been enhanced.

You can't acquire judgment and skill simply by reading books or listening to lectures any more than you can become a great swimmer just by reading a book on swimming. While the knowledge obtained from books and lectures can be valuable, the real gains come from practice at analyzing real business situations.

---

[2]Charles I. Gragg, *Because Wisdom Can't Be Told*, HBS Case No. 9–451–005.

How You Can Get the Most Out of the Process

There are a number of things you can do to get the most out of the process:

1. *Prepare.* Not only is a thorough, individual preparation of each case a great learning experience, it is the key to being an active participant in the case discussion.

2. *Discuss the cases with others beforehand.* As mentioned earlier, this will refine your reasoning. It's not cheating; it's encouraged. However, you'll be cheating yourself if you don't prepare thoroughly before such discussions.

3. *Participate.* In class, actively express your views and challenge others. Learning by talking may seem contrary to how you learned in other settings. You may have been urged to be silent and learn from others, especially the faculty. In case discussions, when you express your views to others you commit which, in turn, gets you involved. This is exactly the same as betting at the racetrack; your bet is a commitment which gets you involved in the race. Talking forces you to decide; you can no longer hedge.

4. *Share your related experience.* During class if you are aware of a situation that relates to the topic being discussed and it would enrich the discussion, tell about it. So-called war stories heighten the relevance of the topic.

5. *Constantly relate the topic and case at hand to your business* no matter how remote the connection seems at first. Don't tune out because of a possible disconnect. You *can* learn *a lot* about marketing insurance by studying a case on marketing razor blades and vice versa. It's not whether it relates, but how.

6. *Actively apply what you are learning to your own, specific management situations, past and future.* That will greatly heighten relevance. Even better is to pick a situation that you know you will face in the future where you could productively use some good ideas. For example, how can I grow my business? Make note of each good idea from the discussion that helps. Not only will these ideas improve the outcome of the situation, they will stick in your mind forever, because they were learned in the context of something important to you.

7. *Note what clicks.* Different people with different backgrounds, experiences, skills and styles will take different things out of the discussions. Your notes will appropriately be quite different from your neighbors'.

8. *Mix it up.* Use the discussion as an opportunity to discover intriguing people with different points of view. Get to know them outside of class and continue your learning there.

9. *Try to better understand and enhance your own management style.* By hearing so many other approaches to a given situation you will be exposed to many styles and thereby understand your own. This understanding will put you in a better position to improve it.

You will learn from rigorous discussion and controversy. Each member of the class—and the instructor—assumes a responsibility for preparing the case and for contributing ideas to the case discussion. The rewards for these responsibilities are a series of highly exciting, practically oriented educational experiences that bring out a wide range of topics and viewpoints.

UVA-E-0318

FACEBOOK (A)

Miranda Shaw was stymied. She had been on the verge of hiring a highly talented recent business school graduate, Rick Parsons, as a senior analyst for her project team. It had been a choice between Parsons and Deborah Jones, another very promising hire. Both Parsons and Jones had graduated from the same highly ranked business school that Shaw had attended, had the appropriate work backgrounds, and had performed well in their multiple rounds of interviews. From their conversations, Shaw believed either one would be a good choice for the company. While she had had a hard time deciding, she was leaning toward hiring Parsons because of his leadership skills and his reputation for tireless energy and great communication skills. Before making her final decision, Shaw—almost in desperation, because she needed to submit her recommendation to human resources immediately—had "Googled" both of the candidates. What she had discovered about Parsons both on-line and at Facebook.com,[1] while not necessarily a deal-breaker, was disturbing enough that she had to rethink her opinion.[2]

Shaw was a manager at a leading consulting firm. She had worked her way up from intern after four years and was on the fast track to making partner. Her company was a special place and as she had seen over the last few years, it took a special type of consultant to work there. She remembered plenty of cases where new hires had left the company in the first few months because they did not fit in with the high-energy and high-commitment work environment. She had seen several projects delayed or worse, because of personnel issues. This high turnover was not good for the company because it invested significant time, energy, and funds to train and mentor new hires. Shaw believed in the adage that "you are only as good as the people who work for you," and she knew that making the right hiring decisions was critical to her success at the firm. Shaw had to take these factors into consideration as she decided between two equally qualified candidates for the position.

---

[1] Facebook is a social networking Web site; see http://www.facebook.com (accessed 7 April 2008).

[2] Facebook's default privacy settings allowed users belonging to the same network to see each other's profiles, which is how Shaw had been able to access Parson's profile.

In her Web search, Shaw was initially impressed with Parsons. He was obviously very involved in nonprofit work and had won a number of community service awards. But she then discovered his Facebook page and found herself quite dismayed. There were several pictures of Parsons with his fraternity brothers; in most, they were drinking, smoking cigarettes, and—in his own words—"smokin' blunts." This term, Shaw learned after a little research, meant smoking cigars hollowed out and stuffed with marijuana.

She then turned her Google efforts to Jones. She did not discover any personal information about Jones, nor did she find Jones on Facebook. There were only work-related sites that listed Jones as an effective project member.

Shaw sighed in dismay. She had been poised, only an hour earlier, to submit her recommendation to hire Parsons. Now she was not sure what to do.

Richard Ivey School of Business
The University of Western Ontario

9B12B030

RAWHIDE BREWERY

Michele Stewart prepared this case solely to provide material for class discussion. The author does not intend to illustrate either effective or ineffective handling of a managerial situation. The author may have disguised certain names and other identifying information to protect confidentiality.

Rawhide Brewery (Rawhide) was an Ontario brewery with annual sales of $5.3 million in 2011. Rawhide had doubled the capacity of its brewery operations in 2009, but sales growth had slowed and the company was currently operating at well below full capacity. The capacity expansion had been financed mainly through a 10-year bank term loan. Andrew Upson, the chief executive officer (CEO), was concerned that carrying the fixed costs of under-utilized capacity was hurting Rawhide's profitability. Sales projections for the next five years showed that full capacity would not likely be achieved within the foreseeable future. Upson was also troubled by the heavy debt burden Rawhide had assumed as a result of the expansion, which was making it difficult for the company to borrow for other purposes. Rawhide's debt-to-equity ratio was well above normal for the industry. Upson had decided to explore the possibility of improving Rawhide's profitability by combining Rawhide's brewery operations with the operations of another brewery.

Tabby Cat Beer (Tabby), a competitor of Rawhide, was a fast-growing Ontario micro-brewery. Tabby had experienced a record year in 2011, as its sales had exceeded $2 million for the first time since it opened for business in 2008. Tabby's rapid growth was mainly attributable to its success in marketing its product line of light and flavourful beer to women. The company's CEO and controlling shareholder, Bruce McAlpine, was very pleased that his company had been able to achieve such an important revenue milestone within three years of commencing operations. He was deeply concerned, however, that the strong revenue growth was putting stress on the company's brewery operations. These operations consisted of manufacturing, bottling and delivery of the beer products to Liquor Control Board of Ontario (LCBO) warehouses, pubs and restaurants. At the time Tabby was formed, such rapid growth had not been anticipated, and the capacity of the company's brewing operations would soon be insufficient to meet demand.

Tabby's brewery operations were located in leased premises. The lease would expire in just under a year; therefore, McAlpine needed to make a decision soon regarding whether to renew the lease. McAlpine had analysed the cost of expanding Tabby's capacity, which would require moving the operations to larger premises. He was concerned that Tabby would need to obtain at least $3 million in debt financing to complete the expansion. Tabby currently had very little debt, and McAlpine, who was quite conservative by nature, was not keen to have his company become highly leveraged.

Upson had heard through contacts within the industry that Tabby was struggling with insufficient capacity, so he invited McAlpine to dinner to broach the subject of working together. He offered McAlpine two proposals.

PROPOSAL #1

Tabby could enter into a five-year contract with Rawhide to outsource all or a portion of its brewery operations to Rawhide for a fee per case of beer. Upson quoted an initial fee, which McAlpine estimated was approximately 20 per cent higher than Tabby's current cost per case. Because of the volatile price of hops, one of the key ingredients in beer, the fee would be adjusted monthly, based on the current price of hops. The amount of the fee would also depend on the Tabby volumes processed by Rawhide, with higher volumes resulting in a lower fee per case. The fee would be adjusted annually for inflation by reference to an established price index. Tabby would need to guarantee that a prescribed minimum number of cases would be processed annually.

PROPOSAL #2

Rawhide would transfer all of its brewery operations and the associated debt financing (the 10-year bank term loan) into a newly formed separate legal entity (Newco). Upson estimated that Rawhide's brewery operations (mainly premises and equipment) had a fair value of $5 million, and the fair value of the outstanding debt was $3.5 million. Tabby would purchase 95 per cent of the common shares of Newco for $950,000, and Rawhide would purchase the remaining 5 per cent for $50,000. Rawhide would transfer ownership of the brewery operations to Newco, and Newco would assume the related bank term loan. In exchange for the transfer of the brewery operations net of the debt, Rawhide would be granted a $1.5 million note receivable due in 10 years. The interest rate on the note would vary depending upon the profitability of Newco. Higher profitability would result in higher interest rates, up to a maximum annual rate of 20 per cent. No interest would be payable in any year in which a loss was incurred by Newco. Under this proposal, both Tabby and Rawhide would process all of their beer production through Newco. Tabby and Rawhide would pay the same fee per case of beer, which would be approximately 15 per cent lower than under Proposal #1. Since Rawhide's bank would require assurance that the term loan transferred to Newco would be repaid, Rawhide would guarantee the term loan. Because, as guarantor, Rawhide would bear the majority of the risk of Newco, Rawhide and Tabby would sign a shareholder agreement giving Rawhide extensive power over decision-making. Upson handed a sheet to McAlpine providing an overview of how decisions would be made (see Exhibit 1).

McAlpine was in a good mood the following morning because he believed he had an opportunity for Tabby to reach an agreement with Rawhide that would resolve Tabby's capacity problem. He quickly wrote down his thoughts on the two proposals put forward by Upson, as follows:

- Combining operations with another brewery, if well-structured, should result in cost savings for both parties, as fixed costs would be spread over a greater production volume.
- The outsourcing proposal (Proposal #1) would result in a significantly higher cost per case of beer than Tabby's current cost, even if virtually all production was outsourced to Rawhide.
- Under Proposal #2, the cost to process a case of beer would be slightly higher than Tabby's current cost but this proposal would enable Tabby to avoid the considerable expenditures that would otherwise need to be incurred to expand Tabby's capacity.

- Outsourcing might lead to loss of control over the production process. Problems such as production delays or poor quality control could tarnish Tabby's brand and hurt revenues.
- Given that Rawhide was a competitor, it might be unwise for Tabby to leave too many key decisions to Rawhide, since this could result in problems such as production delays or poor quality control.
- An investment of approximately $1 million in a combined brewery operation could be undertaken by Tabby without stretching Tabby's leverage to a level beyond which he was uncomfortable.

Since McAlpine had determined that neither of the proposals put forward by Upson was ideal, he decided to make a counter-proposal. Over lunch, he met with Upson and presented him with the following.

COUNTER-PROPOSAL

Similar to Proposal #2, Rawhide would transfer its brewery operations and the associated debt financing (the 10-year bank term loan) to Newco. Rawhide would be granted 60 per cent of Newco's common shares in exchange for its contribution of the brewery operations, net of the debt. Tabby would purchase 40 per cent of Newco's common shares for $1 million. Both Tabby and Rawhide would process all of their beer through Newco, and the fees would be the same as under Proposal #2. Both Tabby and Rawhide would guarantee the term loan. A shareholder agreement would specify that all key decisions (see Exhibit 1) would be discussed and agreed upon by both Rawhide and Tabby. If no consensus could be reached on a particular decision, the shareholder agreement would specify the arbitration procedure to be followed. However, neither shareholder would be able to make a key decision regarding Newco without the agreement of the other.

After receiving McAlpine's counter-proposal, Upson decided it was time to brief Christine Wang, chief financial officer of Rawhide, to get her thoughts on the accounting implications of the various proposals under discussion.

Rawhide's balance sheet and income statement for the year ended December 31, 2011, are provided in Exhibit 2 and Exhibit 3.

Exhibit 1

KEY DECISIONS AFFECTING BREWERY OPERATIONS

Rawhide would be responsible for the following decisions:

- Hiring of management and employees
- Employee compensation arrangements
- Capital expenditures, such as purchases of new equipment
- Relocation or expansion of premises
- Borrowing of additional funds
- Selection of suppliers
- Offering of services to other breweries (i.e. outsourcing arrangements)
- Establishing and changing product delivery schedules

Tabby would be solely responsible for any decisions relating to the formulas for Tabby's beer products.

Tabby would have a veto over any decision to change the supplier from which key ingredients (e.g. hops) were obtained if such a change could significantly alter the quality or taste of Tabby's products.

Tabby would have a veto over any decision to close or significantly reduce the size of the brewery operations.

Exhibit 2

RAWHIDE BREWERY BALANCE SHEET AS AT DECEMBER 31, 2011

(in thousands of Canadian dollars)

ASSETS

Non-current assets

Property, plant and equipment*	$ 5,775
Other	647
	6,422

Current assets

Inventories	403
Accounts receivable	325
Cash and marketable securities	122
Other	165
	1,015
Total assets	$ 7,437

LIABILITIES & SHAREHOLDERS' EQUITY

EQUITY

Common shares	2,220
Retained earnings	969
	3,189

LIABILITIES

Non-current

Long-term debt	3,497
Deferred income taxes	123
	3,620

Current

Accounts payable and accrued liabilities	420
Other	208
	628
Total liabilities & shareholders' equity	$ 7,437

* At cost, net of accumulated depreciation.

Exhibit 3

RAWHIDE BREWERY INCOME STATEMENT FOR THE YEAR ENDED DECEMBER 31, 2011

(in thousands of Canadian dollars)

Net revenue	$ 5,306
Cost of goods sold	3,389
Gross profit	1,917
Marketing, general and administrative expenses	988
Depreciation and amortization	421
Interest expense	226
Other expenses	42
Total expenses	1,677
Net income before income taxes	240
Income tax expense	79
Net income and comprehensive income for the year	$ 161

ARVIND KRISHNAMURTHY AND TAFT FOSTER   **KEL782**

Quantitative Easing in the Great Recession

On October 29, 2008, the Federal Open Market Committee (FOMC) concluded its eighth meeting since the start of the Great Recession eleven months earlier. Continuing its recent pattern, the FOMC voted to cut its target federal funds rate by another 50 basis points, to 1%. Yet despite the lowering of this rate from 4.25% since the start of the year (see **Exhibit 1**), a variety of economic indicators continued to paint a grim picture. Indeed, the situation appeared to be worsening.

The chairman of the U.S. Federal Reserve, Ben Bernanke, now faced a daunting prospect. As a professor of economics at Princeton, Bernanke had studied a set of tools that a central bank could employ if its policy rate were to be constrained by the zero lower bound. Prominent among these was a tool known as "quantitative easing," or QE, a policy of making large purchases of financial assets. These purchases increased the quantity of money in the economy, hence the name *quantitative* easing. In his academic writings, Bernanke had advocated QE as a policy for Japan, where since the late 1990s the Bank of Japan (BoJ) had reduced its short-term interest rate to near zero.[1] With the federal funds rate at 1%, the Federal Reserve likely would soon find itself in the same position as the BoJ, namely at the zero lower bound. Bernanke would get a chance to put his academic theories into practice.

The Great Recession and Financial Crisis

What would later be called the Great Recession began officially in December 2007 as a typical economic downturn associated with a spike in oil prices and a decline in home prices, but it quickly became a severe recession due to links between the housing and financial markets. As home prices across the United States and other countries fell in 2006 and 2007, foreclosure rates began to rise; this in turn rendered almost worthless many previously AAA-rated mortgage-backed securities (MBS) that derived their value from pools of mortgages (see **Exhibit 2** and **Exhibit 3**). In turn, uncertainty about which financial institutions held worthless MBS—and which financial institutions insured the losses of those that did—caused what amounted to bank runs on several large financial institutions.

---

[1] See Ben Bernanke, "Japanese Monetary Policy: A Case of Self-Induced Paralysis?" in Ryoichi Mikitani and Adam Simon Posen, eds., *Japan's Financial Crisis and Its Parallels to U.S. Experience* (Washington, DC: Institute for International Economics, 2000).

Early notable victims included Countrywide Financial, which reached a deal in January 2008 to be purchased by Bank of America, and Northern Rock, which was nationalized by the British government in February 2008. Both were heavily involved in mortgage lending and unable to obtain financing through credit markets. Then, on March 16, 2008, the FOMC held an emergency meeting in response to the imminent collapse of Bear Stearns, at that time the fifth largest investment bank in the United States. During that meeting, the Federal Reserve pledged financing for J.P. Morgan to purchase Bear Stearns at $2 per share, less than 7% of Bear Stearns's market value two days earlier. Six months later, another large investment bank, Lehman Brothers, faced a similar crisis. This time, however, the Federal Reserve was unable or unwilling to provide a bailout, and no buyer could be found. As a result, Lehman Brothers, the fourth largest U.S. investment bank at the time, filed for Chapter 11 bankruptcy protection on September 15, 2008.

On the day of Lehman's bankruptcy filing, the Dow Jones Industrial Average plummeted 500 points (-4.4%), its largest decline since the attacks of September 11, 2001. Lehman's downfall created widespread panic in financial markets, as investors scrambled to move their funds out of other potentially at-risk institutions and investments. The multinational insurance giant AIG suffered a liquidity crisis the day after Lehman's bankruptcy filing. This time, however, the Federal Reserve stepped in to prevent the collapse of AIG by providing a secured credit facility of up to $85 billion. This was followed a week later by the federal takeover of Fannie Mae and Freddie Mac, government-sponsored enterprises (GSEs) that securitized mortgages in the form of MBS. **Exhibit 4** shows the magnitude of financial institution write-downs throughout this period.

By the time the FOMC met on October 29, the Dow Jones had dropped more than 2,300 points, or 20.6%, since Lehman's bankruptcy. Meanwhile, the turmoil in the financial sector was also being felt in the real economy. According to the Federal Reserve's October 2008 Senior Loan Officer Opinion Survey, credit standards were tightening sharply (see **Exhibit 5**). Real GDP fell 3.7% during the third quarter of 2008 and the unemployment rate, which was on a sharp upward trajectory, reached 6.5% in October, up from 5% at the start of the recession (see **Exhibit 6**).

Quantitative Easing

As the economic situation continued to deteriorate following the October 29 FOMC meeting, it became clear that the Federal Reserve would soon be forced to lower its target rate further. With the target rate already at 1%, however, the Federal Reserve did not have much room for further easing. Monetary policy would soon be constrained by the zero lower bound.

The Zero Lower Bound

One way to look at the zero lower bound is through the lens of the Taylor rule. Named after its creator, Stanford economist John Taylor, this mathematical formula indicates how much a central bank should adjust its policy rate in response to changes in inflation, output, or unemployment. More specifically, Taylor proposed the following equation:

$$i_t = r_t^* + \pi_t + \beta_\pi(\pi_t - \pi_t^*) + \beta_y(y_t - \bar{y}_t)$$

KEL782   QUANTITATIVE EASING

Applying this equation to the United States, i_t represents the federal funds rate, r_t^* is the equilibrium real interest rate, π_t is the inflation rate, π_t^* is the Federal Reserve's target inflation rate, y_t is the logarithm of real GDP, and $\bar{y}_t$ is the logarithm of potential output. The coefficients β_π and β_y tell the Federal Reserve how much to adjust the federal funds rate in response to deviations in the inflation rate from its target and to deviations in real GDP from potential output.[2]

From 1988 to 2007, under first Alan Greenspan and then Ben Bernanke, the Federal Reserve had set the federal funds rate in a manner that could be described by a modified Taylor rule (see Exhibit 1). The main difference between Taylor's rule and actual Federal Reserve policy was that Taylor proposed, in a paper published in 1993, that the Federal Reserve choose β_π equal to one-half and β_y equal to one-half, whereas the Federal Reserve appeared to choose β_y to be closer to one.[3]

Beginning in late 2008, the Federal Reserve's modified Taylor rule began to recommend a negative federal funds rate, something that was impossible to implement. This constraint on the federal funds rate is a consequence of the fact that investors can always earn at least a 0% nominal return by holding cash. As a result, banks will almost never be willing to lend reserves at a rate below 0%, that is, to pay to lend reserves. So, according to the modified Taylor rule, by late 2008, Federal Reserve policy was constrained by the zero lower bound.

Although new to the Federal Reserve, the zero lower bound was familiar territory for Japan's central bank, the BoJ. In 1995 the BoJ had dropped its target rate below 1% in an attempt to combat deflation and a stagnant economy. This rate remained close to zero for several years, but Japan's Lost Decade continued unabated. So in 2001, under pressure to do something more to stimulate the Japanese economy, the BoJ became the world's first central bank to try quantitative easing. Among those calling for increased use of quantitative easing in Japan at that time was Ben Bernanke, then a Princeton economics professor.[4] Seven years later, Bernanke had the opportunity to put his theories to the test in the United States.

QE1

On November 25, 2008, the Federal Reserve issued a press release announcing plans to purchase up to $600 billion in financial assets in what would later be referred to as QE1. Of these funds, $500 billion would be used to purchase MBS backed by Fannie Mae, Freddie Mac, and Ginnie Mae. The remaining $100 billion would go to purchase direct obligations (i.e., plain vanilla bonds rather than MBS) of Fannie Mae, Freddie Mac, and the Federal Home Loan Banks.

Over the next four months, the Federal Reserve made four more announcements regarding quantitative easing. On December 1, Bernanke gave a speech in which he described "several

---

[2] The Taylor rule is sometimes written in terms of unemployment gaps rather than GDP gaps, appealing to Okun's law relating GDP gap deviations to unemployment deviations. In this case, the last term in the Taylor rule is modified from $\beta_y(y_t - \bar{y}_t)$ to $-\beta_u(u_t - \bar{u}_t)$, where u_t is the unemployment rate and $\bar{u}_t$ is the natural rate of unemployment.

[3] See John B. Taylor, "Discretion versus Policy Rules in Practice," *Carnegie-Rochester Conference Series on Public Policy* 39 (1993): 195–214, and John B. Taylor, "A Historical Analysis of Monetary Policy Rules," in *Monetary Policy Rules* (Chicago: University of Chicago Press, 1999), pp. 319–41.

[4] See Ben Bernanke, "Japanese Monetary Policy: A Case of Self-Induced Paralysis?" in Ryoichi Mikitani and Adam Simon Posen, eds., *Japan's Financial Crisis and Its Parallels to U.S. Experience* (Washington, DC: Institute for International Economics, 2000).

---

means by which the Fed could influence financial conditions through the use of its balance sheet," including purchases of "longer-term Treasury or agency securities on the open market in substantial quantities."[5] Then, on December 16, the FOMC lowered its target federal funds rate to 0%–0.25%, essentially hitting the zero lower bound. The press release for this meeting also stated that the Federal Reserve stood "ready to expand its purchases of agency debt and mortgage-backed securities as conditions warrant" and was "also evaluating the potential benefits of purchasing longer-term Treasury securities."[6] Similar comments were made after the subsequent FOMC meeting held on January 28.[7] Finally, on March 18, the Federal Reserve expanded QE1 to include $1.25 trillion in MBS purchases and $300 billion in long-term Treasury purchases.

Although it is impossible to fully identify the effects of QE1 on the economy, some insight about its effects can be obtained using an event study methodology.[8] With this approach, key variables are observed shortly before and after each of the five announcements described above. To the degree that these announcements represented the dominant news affecting the market on their respective dates, changes in certain variables around the announcements can shed light on the channels through which QE1 operated, as well as its overall impact. Intraday movements in 10-year Treasury yields and trading volume for each of the event dates provide evidence that the five announcements were indeed the major piece of news on their respective dates (see **Exhibit 7**). Further evidence for the effects of QE1 can be found in **Table 1** below, which displays the two-day changes in the yields of several securities summed across the five event dates. **Table 2** contains this same information for federal funds futures at various maturities; the average yield curve before and after the five announcements provide additional evidence (see **Exhibit 8**).

Table 1: Changes in Yields (in Basis Points) on Select Securities

	QE1	QE2
5-year Treasuries	-74	-17
10-year Treasuries	-107	-18
Agency MBS (10-year duration)	-107	-12
Baa Corporate Yield	-81	-7
Credit Default Swap[a]	-40	2
10-year TIPS	-187	-25

[a] The credit default swap yield in this table corresponds to an index of Baa corporates.

Table 2: Changes in Yields (in Basis Points) on Federal Funds Futures by Maturity

	QE1	QE2
3rd month	-28	0
6th month	-27	-1
12th month	-33	-4
24th month	-40	-11

---

[5] Ben S. Bernanke, "Federal Reserve Policies in the Financial Crisis," speech at the Greater Austin Chamber of Commerce, Austin, Texas, December 1, 2008, http://www.federalreserve.gov/newsevents/speech/bernanke20081201a.htm.

[6] Board of Governors of the Federal Reserve System, press release, December 16, 2008, http://www.federalreserve.gov/newsevents/press/monetary/20081216b.htm.

[7] Board of Governors of the Federal Reserve System, press release, January 28, 2009, http://www.federalreserve.gov/newsevents/press/monetary/20090128a.htm.

[8] See Arvind Krishnamurthy and Annette Vissing-Jorgensen, "The Effects of Quantitative Easing on Interest Rates: Channels and Implications for Policy," Brookings Papers on Economic Activity, Fall 2011.

QE1 was executed over a period of sixteen months and concluded when the last of its purchases were made during March 2010. By that time, the U.S. economy was no longer in free fall, but the unemployment rate was 9.9% and the recovery appeared to be proceeding at a slow pace. Meanwhile, dark clouds were forming over Europe, which was showing early signs of a sovereign debt crisis. After months of sluggish recovery and talk of a "double-dip recession," Wall Street began to speculate about QE2.

QE2

The first official hint of QE2 came on August 10, 2010, when the FOMC announced its plan to "keep constant the Federal Reserve's holdings of securities at their current level by reinvesting principal payments from agency debt and agency mortgage-backed securities in longer-term Treasury securities."[9] Prior to this announcement, markets had expected the Federal Reserve to gradually reduce its balance sheet. The announcement indicated a shift toward long-term Treasuries and away from MBS, which had been the focus of QE1. The next FOMC announcement on September 21 reaffirmed this position and added that the committee was "prepared to provide additional accommodation if needed to support the economic recovery."[10] This language was interpreted by many market participants as signaling a new round of asset purchases by the Federal Reserve. For example, Goldman Sachs economists forecasted that the Federal Reserve would purchase up to $1 trillion of Treasuries.[11] As a result of these widespread expectations, markets were underwhelmed when, on November 3, the FOMC finally announced its plan to purchase $600 billion in long-term Treasuries.

Applying the event study approach to QE2, there are three possible dates to work with, but because the November 3 announcement was largely priced into the market beforehand, only the August 10 and September 21 announcements are included in the data provided here. Intraday movements in 10-year Treasury yields and trading volumes provide evidence that the QE2 announcements were the major news event on their respective release dates (see **Exhibit 9**). As with QE1, further evidence can be found in the changes in security yields and the yields on federal funds futures (see Tables 1 and 2), and the average yield curve before and after the announcements provide additional evidence (see **Exhibit 10**).

QE3

On September 13, 2012, the Federal Reserve launched QE3. It was announced that the Federal Reserve would purchase MBS at a pace of $40 billion per month, and it would purchase longer-term Treasury securities at a pace of $45 billion per month. The Treasury purchases were for the most part expected, but the announcement of MBS purchases took the market by surprise. It indicated a shift back toward MBS, unlike the exclusive focus on Treasury securities in QE2. Of further surprise was the Federal Reserve's indication that purchases would continue until the

---

[9] Board of Governors of the Federal Reserve System, press release, August 10, 2010, http://www.federalreserve.gov/newsevents/press/monetary/20100810a.htm.

[10] Board of Governors of the Federal Reserve System, press release, September 21, 2010, http://www.federalreserve.gov/newsevents/press/monetary/20100921a.htm.

[11] "FOMC Rate Decision—Fed Signals Willingness to Ease Further if Growth or Inflation Continue to Disappoint," Goldman Sachs Newsletter, September 21, 2010.

labor market improved, within the context of price stability. The press release stated, "If the outlook for the labor market does not improve substantially, the Committee will continue its purchases of agency mortgage-backed securities, undertake additional asset purchases, and employ its other policy tools as appropriate until such improvement is achieved in a context of price stability."[12] The open-ended nature of this purchase commitment led some commentators to dub QE3 as "QE infinity."[13]

Table 3: Changes in Yields (in Basis Points) on Select Securities

	QE3
5-year Treasuries	-6
10-year Treasuries	-3
Agency MBS (10-year duration)	-15
Baa Corporate Yield	0
Credit Default Swap[a]	0
10-year TIPS	-11

[a] The credit default swap yield in this table corresponds to an investment grade index.

Table 4: Changes in Yields (in Basis Points) on Federal Funds Futures by Maturity

	QE3
3rd month	0
6th month	0
12th month	0
24th month	-3

The event study for QE3 involves only one clear-cut surprise date, the announcement date of September 13, 2012. **Table 3** and **Table 4** provide data on the one-day change in asset prices across the event date.[14]

The QE Debate

Although Bernanke had been a longtime proponent of quantitative easing and the majority of FOMC members agreed that QE1, QE2, and QE3 were merited, committee members held a wide range of views regarding the policy. Much of the debate surrounded the potential costs and benefits of the Federal Reserve's actions.

---

[12] Board of Governors of the Federal Reserve System, press release, September 13, 2012, http://www.federalreserve.gov/newsevents/ press/monetary/20120913a.htm.

[13] Sam Jones, "Hedge Fund Sceptics Warn on 'QE Infinity,'" *Financial Times*, September 25, 2012.

[14] See Arvind Krishnamurthy and Annette Vissing-Jorgensen, "The Ins and Outs of Large Scale Asset Purchases," Federal Reserve Bank of Kansas City Economic Symposium on the Global Dimensions of Unconventional Monetary Policy, Jackson Hole, Wyoming, August 2013.

KEL782   QUANTITATIVE EASING

Potential Benefits of QE

Janet Yellen, former president of the Federal Reserve Bank of San Francisco and vice chairwoman of the Federal Reserve, was a vocal supporter of quantitative easing. In a January 2011 speech defending the Federal Reserve's decision to proceed with QE2, she described the policy's potential benefits:

> *Turning now to the macroeconomic effects of the Federal Reserve's securities purchases, there are several distinct channels through which these purchases tend to influence aggregate demand, including a reduced cost of credit to consumers and businesses, a rise in asset prices that boosts household wealth and spending, and a moderate change in the foreign exchange value of the dollar that provides support to net exports.*[15]

She also cited the results of the Federal Reserve's forecasting model, which predicted that by 2012, "the full program of securities purchases will have raised private payroll employment by about 3 million jobs."[16]

In an October 2010 speech, William Dudley, president of the Federal Reserve Bank of New York and another of the FOMC's so-called inflation doves,[17] emphasized the effects of quantitative easing through the mortgage-rate and business-lending channels:

> *Lower long-term rates would make housing more affordable and support consumption by enabling households to refinance their mortgages at lower rates. This would increase the amount of income left over for other spending. Of course, this channel can be made more powerful to the extent that further progress can be made in efficient mortgage debt restructurings that allow households with negative equity in their homes to take advantage of the drop in mortgage rates. In addition, lower long-term rates would reduce the cost of capital for businesses, thereby fostering higher levels of capital spending for any given economic outlook.*[18]

In addition to the channels emphasized in these speeches, Chairman Bernanke also described the signaling channel of quantitative easing:

> *Large-scale asset purchases . . . can signal that the central bank intends to pursue a persistently more accommodative policy stance than previously thought, thereby lowering*

---

[15] Janet L. Yellen, "The Federal Reserve's Asset Purchase Program," speech at the The Brimmer Policy Forum, Allied Social Science Associations Annual Meeting, Denver, Colorado, January 8, 2011, http://www.federalreserve.gov/newsevents/speech/yellen20110108a.htm.

[16] Ibid.

[17] The Federal Reserve has a dual mandate to create high employment and keep inflation low. The term "dove" is used to indicate a policymaker who places a greater weight on high employment in this dual mandate, while the term "hawk" is used to indicate a policymaker who places a greater weight on inflation.

[18] William C. Dudley, "The Outlook, Policy Choices and Our Mandate," speech at the Society of American Business Editors and Writers Fall Conference, City University of New York, Graduate School of Journalism, New York City, October 1, 2010, http://www.newyorkfed.org/newsevents/speeches/2010/dud101001.html.

---

investors' expectations for the future path of the federal funds rate and putting additional downward pressure on long-term interest rates, particularly in real terms.[19]

Furthermore, Bernanke pointed out that during periods of financial crisis like that of late 2008, "asset purchases may also improve the functioning of financial markets, thereby easing credit conditions in some sectors."[20]

Potential Costs of QE

In a November 2010 speech, Richard Fisher, president of the Federal Reserve Bank of Dallas and one of the FOMC's so-called inflation hawks, described the doubts he had about QE2:

> *I could not state with conviction that purchasing another several hundred billion dollars of Treasuries—on top of the amount we were already committed to buy in order to compensate for the run-off in our $1.25 trillion portfolio of mortgage-backed securities— would lead to job creation and final-demand-spurring behavior. But I could envision such action would lead to a declining dollar, encourage further speculation, provoke commodity hoarding, accelerate the transfer of wealth from the deliberate saver and the unfortunate, and possibly place at risk the stature and independence of the Fed.*[21]

In February 2013, Federal Reserve Governor Jeremy Stein gave a speech on what he saw as overheating in the credit markets. **Exhibit 11** and **Exhibit 12**, which are figures referred to in Stein's speech, show that inflows into high-yield mutual funds, high-yield exchange traded funds (ETFs), and real-estate investment trusts (REITs) had surged from 2010 onward. Commenting on these market developments, Stein noted:

> *. . . a prolonged period of low interest rates, of the sort we are experiencing today, can create incentives for agents to take on greater duration or credit risks, or to employ additional financial leverage, in an effort to "reach for yield." An insurance company that has offered guaranteed minimum rates of return on some of its products might find its solvency threatened by a long stretch of low rates and feel compelled to take on added risk. A similar logic applies to a bank whose net interest margins are under pressure because low rates erode the profitability of its deposit-taking franchise . . .*[22]

In a December 2010 speech, Charles Plosser, president of the Federal Reserve Bank of Philadelphia, expressed concerns about the Federal Reserve's ability to reduce its balance sheet without stoking inflation:

> *While the high level of excess reserves is not inflationary now, as the economic recovery strengthens, the Fed must be able to remove or isolate these reserves to keep them from*

---

[19] Ben S. Bernanke, "Monetary Policy since the Onset of the Crisis," speech at the Federal Reserve Bank of Kansas City Economic Symposium, Jackson Hole, Wyoming, August 31, 2012, http://www.federalreserve.gov/newsevents/speech/bernanke20120831a.htm.
[20] Ibid.
[21] Richard W. Fisher, remarks before the Association for Financial Professionals, San Antonio, Texas, November 8, 2010, http://dallasfed.org/news/speeches/fisher/2010/fs101108.cfm.
[22] Jeremy C. Stein, "Overheating in Credit Markets: Origins, Measurement, and Policy Responses," speech at the Federal Reserve Bank of St. Louis, St. Louis, Missouri, February 7, 2013, http://www.federalreserve.gov/newsevents/speech/stein20130207a.htm.

becoming what I have called the kindling that could fuel excessive inflation. In other words, if banks began to put the reserves to use in the same manner as they did before the crisis, money in circulation would increase sharply. We do not know when that will happen or how long it will take for the banking system to make the adjustment. To address this looming challenge, the Fed is developing and testing tools to help us prevent such a rapid explosion in money. But, of course, we won't know for certain how effective these new tools are until we need to use them in our exit strategy.[23]

Exhibit 13 plots the monetary base (M0), which includes bank reserves as well as currency in circulation. Plosser's concern regarding the high level of bank reserves is reflected in the rapid growth of M0. As Plosser notes, broader measures of money in circulation such as M2 (see Exhibit 11) have not kept pace with M0, indicating that banks have not put the reserves to use. **Exhibit 14** plots the yields on 10-year nominal Treasury bonds and 10-year Treasury inflation indexed bonds (TIPS). The difference between the yields in these series can be used to measure long-term inflation expectations.

Plosser also pointed out the fact that "the Federal Reserve also faces interest rate risk by purchasing these long-term government bonds. If rates go up and the Fed were forced to sell the bonds in order to prevent inflation, the Fed would take a loss."[24]

In a March 2009 speech, Jeffrey Lacker, president of the Federal Reserve Bank of Richmond, described his view that recent Federal Reserve actions put the central bank's political independence at risk:

Government lending, whether by the Fed or by the Treasury, fundamentally represents fiscal policy in the sense that it channels taxpayer funds to private sector entities. The presumption ought to be that such lending is subject to the checks and balances of the appropriations process laid out in the Constitution. Using the Fed's balance sheet is at times the path of least resistance, because it allows government lending to circumvent the Congressional approval process. This risks entangling the Fed in attempts to influence credit allocation, thereby exposing monetary policy to political pressures.[25]

Table 5: Holdings of Agency MBS and US Treasury Debt, by Holder ($ in billions)

	Agency MBS		Treasury (1–5 yr)		Treasury (>5 yr)	
	Fed	Non-Fed	Fed	Non-Fed	Fed	Non-Fed
30-Jun-08	0	4,756	173	1,389	183	1,275
30-Jun-12	947	4,656	516	3,710	1,092	2,335
30-Jun-13	1,208	4,547	552	4,125	1,382	2,392

Source: Federal Reserve, U.S. Treasury, SIFMA.

---

[23] Charles I. Plosser, "Economic Outlook and Monetary Policy," speech at the 32nd Annual Economic Seminar, Rochester, New York, December 2, 2010, http://www.philadelphiafed.org/publications/speeches/plosser/2010/12-02-10_university-of-rochester.cfm.

[24] Ibid.

[25] Jeffrey M. Lacker, "Government Lending and Monetary Policy," speech at the 2009 National Association for Business Economics Economic Policy Conference, Alexandria, Virginia, March 2, 2009, http://www.richmondfed.org/press_room/speeches/president_jeff_lacker/2009/lacker_speech_20090302.cfm.

As of the summer of 2013, the Federal Reserve's actions in the MBS and Treasury market were substantial relative to the size of these markets. **Table 5** provides data on the Federal Reserve and private sector's (i.e., non-Fed) holdings of long maturity U.S. Treasury debt, broken down into Treasury bonds with one- to five-year maturity and bonds with greater than five-year maturity. The table also provides data on the holdings of Agency MBS. As the table shows, the Federal Reserve was substantially invested in these markets, and these numbers begged the question of how much involvement was too much.

KEL782   QUANTITATIVE EASING

Definitions

CREDIT DEFAULT SWAPS

A credit default swap (CDS) is a financial derivative contract between two parties. The seller of the CDS agrees to compensate the buyer in the event that a third party defaults on a loan or debt obligation. In return, the buyer makes a series of payments to the seller. For a buyer who is also the holder of the specified loan, a CDS provides insurance against default; however, buyers of CDS contracts are not required to hold the loan in question. A CDS in which the buyer has no direct insurable interest is referred to as a "naked" CDS. Given their insurance value, CDS yields are often used as a measure of credit risk.

For example, let us suppose that the CDS price for five years of protection against default on the senior debt of Bank A trades at 1%. This means that to insure against default on $1,000 face value of senior debt of Bank A, the buyer of the CDS pays an insurance premium of 1% × $1,000 = $10 annually. Suppose an investor purchases $1,000 of the senior debt of Bank A at par and offering a yield of 5%. Then, if the investor further purchases the CDS against the default on this debt, the investor will effectively own a riskless bond whose return is equal to 4% (i.e., 5% − 1%). Thus, the 1% CDS price measures the credit or default risk on this bond.

FEDERAL FUNDS FUTURES

Federal funds futures are standardized, exchange-traded derivative contracts. In order to describe this contract, let $\bar{r}$ denote the average value of the daily effective federal funds rate over some future month, and let F denote the current federal funds futures rate for contracts settled at the end of that month. The buyer of a federal funds futures contract that matures at the end of the month in question must compensate the seller if it turns out that $\bar{r} > F$, and vice versa if $F > \bar{r}$. Because federal funds futures represent bets on the value of the federal funds rate at different time horizons, they are often used to gauge market expectations about future Federal Reserve policy.

Exhibit 1: Actual Federal Funds Rate and Taylor Rules, 1988–2014

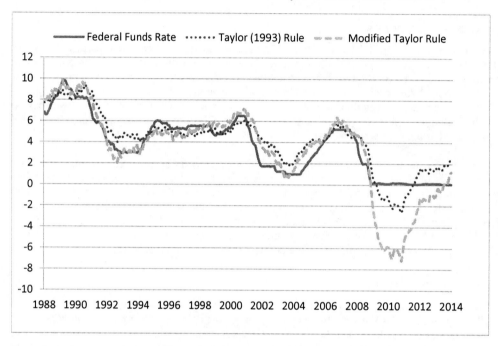

Source: Federal Reserve Bank of St. Louis Economic Data, Congressional Budget Office.

Note: The Taylor rules in this chart are based on:

$$i_t = r_t^* + \pi_t + \beta_\pi(\pi_t - \pi_t^*) + \beta_u(\bar{u}_t - u_t)$$

where the output term has been replaced with $\beta_u(\bar{u}_t - u_t)$, following footnote 2 and an Okun's law estimate of the relationship between the output gap and unemployment of one-half. The original rule proposed by John Taylor in Taylor (1993) sets β_π equal to one-half and β_u equal to one. The modified Taylor rule sets β_π equal to one-half and β_u equal to two. The data for the chart is based on unemployment and core CPI inflation. The inflation target (π_t^*) is assumed to be 2%; the natural rate of interest (r_t^*) is assumed to be 2%; and the natural rate of unemployment ($\bar{u}_t$) is based on the Congressional Budget Office's quarterly estimates.

Exhibit 2: S&P/Case-Shiller Ten-City Index of Home Prices, 2000–2013

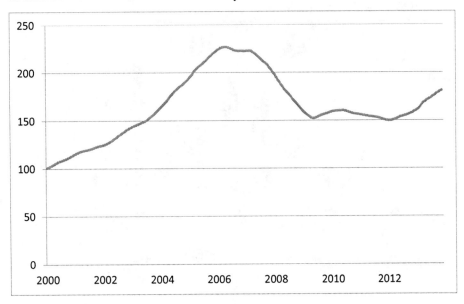

Source: Federal Reserve Bank of St. Louis Economic Data

Note: Indexed to 100 in 2000.

Exhibit 3: Percentage of Homeowners with Negative Equity

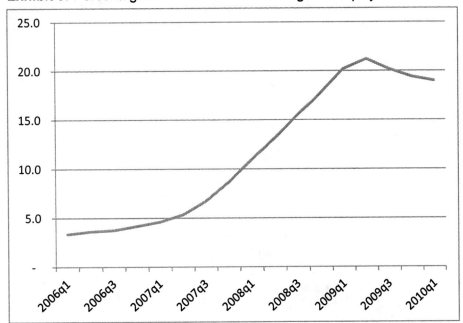

Sources: FDIC, Equifax, Moody's Analytics.

QUANTITATIVE EASING   **KEL782**

Exhibit 4: U.S. Financial Institutions (Banks/Brokers, Insurance, Monolines) Writedowns and Capital Raised (billions of dollars)

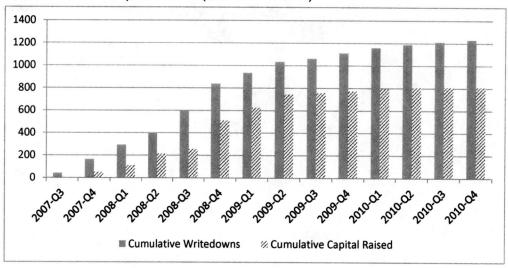

Source: Bloomberg.

KEL782

Exhibit 5: Lending Standards for Mortgage and Consumer Loans, 2000–2014

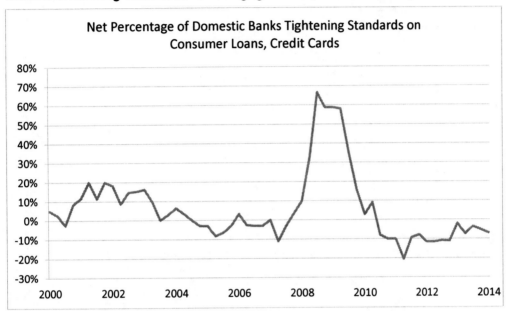

Source: Federal Reserve Bank of St. Louis Economic Data.

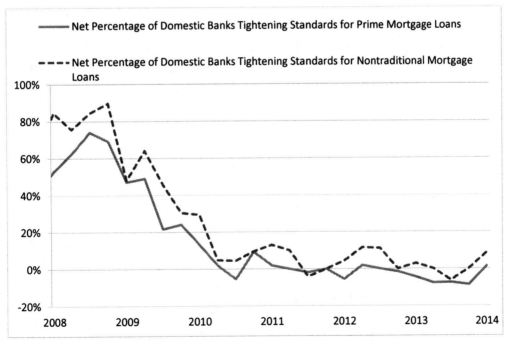

Source: Federal Reserve Bank of St. Louis Economic Data.

Exhibit 6: U.S. Macroeconomic Data

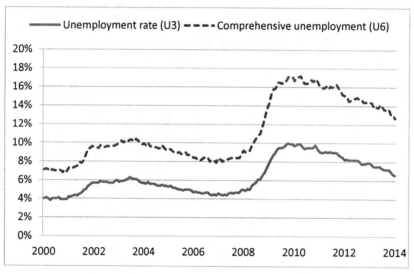

Source: Federal Reserve Bank of St. Louis Economic Data.

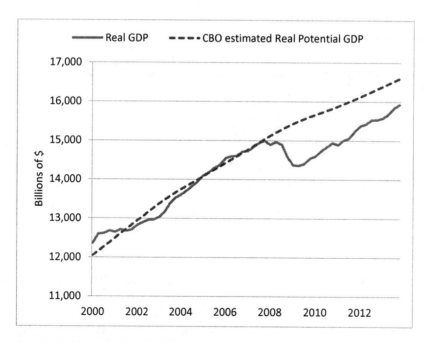

Source: Federal Reserve Bank of St. Louis Economic Data, Congressional Budget Office.

Exhibit 7: 10-Year Treasury Yields and Trading Volumes on the Five QE1 Event Dates

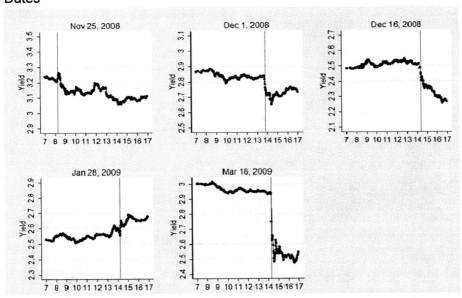

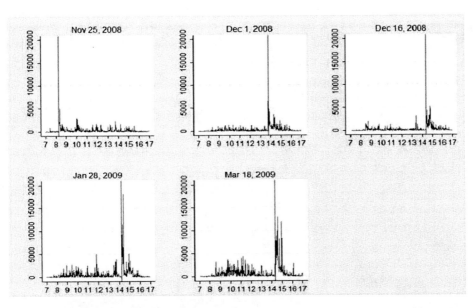

Source: Arvind Krishnamurthy and Annette Vissing-Jorgensen, "The Effects of Quantitative Easing on Interest Rates: Channels and Implications for Policy," Brookings Papers on Economic Activity, Fall 2011.

Note: The x-axis gives time of day, with the vertical lines marking the event time corresponding to a QE announcement. The top panel graphs 10-year Treasury yields over the trading day, while the bottom panel graphs trading volume in the 10-year Treasury bond over the trading day.

QUANTITATIVE EASING   **KEL782**

Exhibit 8: Pre- and Post-QE1 Announcement Average Yield Curve from Federal Funds Futures

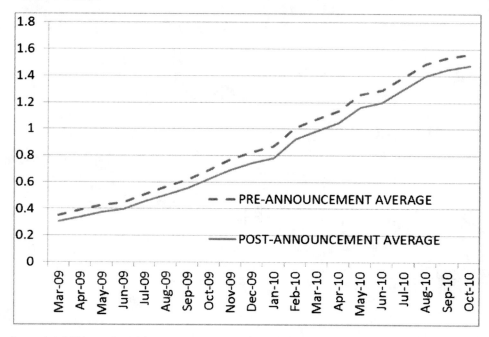

Source: Arvind Krishnamurthy and Annette Vissing-Jorgensen, "The Effects of Quantitative Easing on Interest Rates: Channels and Implications for Policy," Brookings Papers on Economic Activity, Fall 2011.

Exhibit 9: 10-Year Treasury Yields and Trading Volumes on the Two QE2 Event Dates

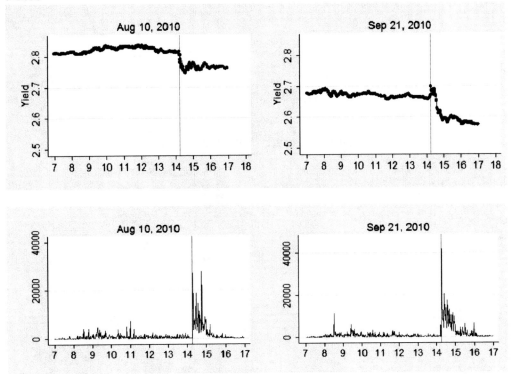

Source: Arvind Krishnamurthy and Annette Vissing-Jorgensen, "The Effects of Quantitative Easing on Interest Rates: Channels and Implications for Policy," Brookings Papers on Economic Activity, Fall 2011.

Note: The x-axis gives time of day, with the vertical lines marking the event time corresponding to a QE announcement. The top panel graphs 10-year Treasury yields over the trading day, while the bottom panel graphs trading volume in the 10-year Treasury bond over the trading day.

Exhibit 10: Pre- and Post-QE2 Announcement Average Yield Curve from Federal Funds Futures

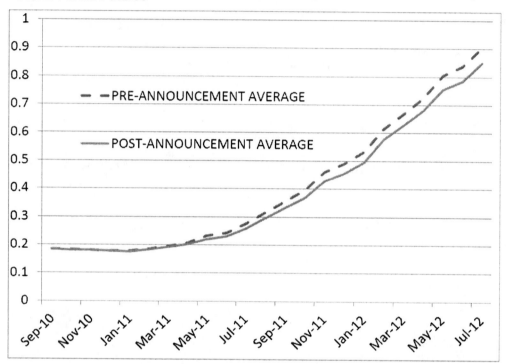

Source: Arvind Krishnamurthy and Annette Vissing-Jorgensen, "The Effects of Quantitative Easing on Interest Rates: Channels and Implications for Policy," Brookings Papers on Economic Activity, Fall 2011.

KEL782

Exhibit 11: Credit Market Inflows, 2000–2012

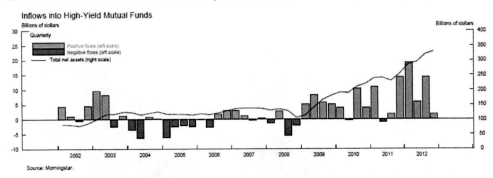

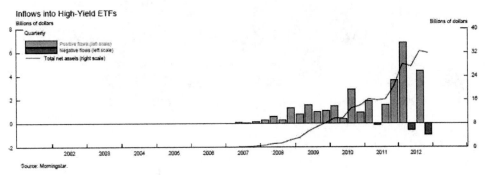

Source: Jeremy C. Stein, "Overheating in Credit Markets: Origins, Measurement, and Policy Responses," speech at the Federal Reserve Bank of St. Louis, St. Louis, Missouri, February 7, 2013, http://www.federalreserve.gov/newsevents/speech/stein20130207a.htm, from Morningstar.

QUANTITATIVE EASING   KEL782

Exhibit 12: Mortgage REIT Assets, 2000–2013 (billions of dollars)

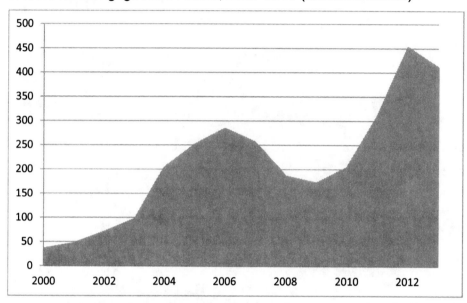

Source: Federal Reserve Financial Accounts of the United States.

Exhibit 13: Money Supply Measures, 2000–2014

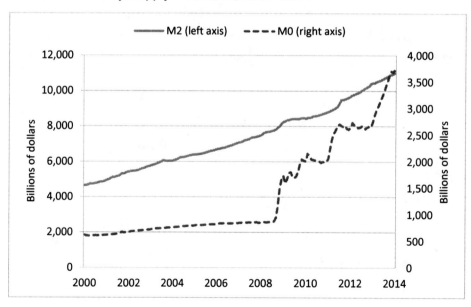

Source: Federal Reserve Bank of St. Louis Economic Data.

QUANTITATIVE EASING

Exhibit 14: Yields on Nominal Treasury Bonds and Inflation Protected Treasury
Bonds, 2003–2014

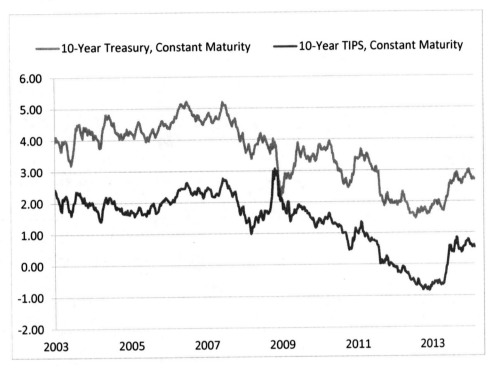

Source: Federal Reserve Bank of St. Louis Economic Data.

IVEY | Publishing

9B14E008

HUSTREAM TECHNOLOGIES INTERACTIVE VIDEO

Laura Marcolin wrote this case under the supervision of Professors Barbara Marcolin, Kathryn Brohman, Ning Su and Norine Webster solely to provide material for class discussion. The authors do not intend to illustrate either effective or ineffective handling of a managerial situation. The authors may have disguised certain names and other identifying information to protect confidentiality.

Version: 2014-04-29

Marlee Lawrence, head of a management consulting team, had been hired to advise HuStream Technologies Inc. (HuStream) co-founders, Peter Matejcek, chief executive officer (CEO), and Amy Matejcek, chief operating officer (COO), on a new business model and target market. HuStream operated on a services-based business model, providing customers with fully produced interactive video content. In the co-founders' efforts to transition to a product-based business, they had built a cloud-based platform to provide easy accessibility to their firm's products and services. Using that platform, clients were able to produce their own interactive content on the web. However, HuStream was facing lagging results because of the difficulty of balancing a services-based business model with a products-based business model.

The task for Lawrence and her team, a total of five consultants with varying skill sets, was to recommend the industries that represented HuStream's top business and market opportunities. The team needed to provide HuStream with convincing evidence of potential new business models and specific vertical opportunities, in the effort to create future business and revenue models to ensure the firm's success going forward. Lawrence and her consulting team were one of several consultancies pitching recommendations to HuStream. Lawrence and her team needed to consider the many options, weigh them against other solutions, and then develop a set of recommendations and supporting action plans for HuStream to enter each industry.

CURRENT SITUATION

HuStream operated its global business operations on the Internet using a cloud-based platform, which allowed its customers increased access, ease of use and convenience, as they built their interactive material flexibly as they saw fit. Clients logged into the cloud and created content that was based on their own needs. Given the cloud was protected by SSL (Secure Sockets Layer) security, critical protection was ensured.

Interactive video content demonstrated evolving platforms in the online service-based business industry, where new features and functionality provided customers and users with unique experiences, on which HuStream customers could put their own stamp. For instance, in the education industry, HuStream's university and college clients were able to provide customized buttons on their schools' websites that students could use to receive a tailored experience; students with a short attention span could receive a broader and shorter experience within 45 seconds. HuStream had developed this metric from its initial customers and knew it was a key success factor.

HuStream was a hub for video production, providing high-quality video production services for clients through an in-house studio equipped with top-performing camera equipment. HuStream believed that producing quality video should be inexpensive, which is why it provided cost-effective options for the production of their customers' video content. Using a team of skilled professionals, HuStream produced quality video services at an affordable cost:

> We have a proven process to video production that is guaranteed to be smoother and more efficient then you probably think. We begin with Scope and Discovery where we establish needs, goals, timing, and budget. Once the plan for the video is laid out, we work with you to ensure the video messaging is aligned with your marketing and goals. When we are all confident that the Pre-Production is tight we let the cameras roll. Regardless of where and how the footage is shot, our Production team is world class and will absolutely ensure that the capture is top shelf. Your project then moves on to Post Production where the footage is edited and visuals and graphics are added. Finally, your video is ready for Launch and we work very closely with you on an effective launch strategy to maximize traffic to your video and make sure it gets seen![1]

HuStream produced a wide variety of video content. Since video conveyed a quick information transfer, the market for interactive video content was potentially vast, which led to HuStream offering many different types of video production services to attract a varying customer base, including promotions and advertising, corporate videos, software demonstrations, commercials and YouTube, student recruitment, instructional and training, guided selling with calls to action, self-help and FAQs (frequently asked questions) and customer testimonials. Peter Matejcek believed the current HuStream revenue represented a small portion of the untapped market in interactive content, but that combining HuStream's current skills with new emerging business models would enable HuStream to expand and diversify in any direction identified as profitable.

Due to HuStream's philosophy and commitment to quality, and despite its short time in business, the firm had already worked with some prestigious clients, securing such well-established, global companies as Microsoft and Intel, in addition to many educational institutions in the firm's local region of Kelowna, British Columbia, Canada. Working with companies with the calibre of Microsoft and Intel had given HuStream credibility, enabling the company to expand production more rapidly. In the future, quickly increasing HuStream's production ability and services-based business platform would create a large capital requirement, which would make it difficult to expand quickly and capture market share. The company needed to be able to better manage its ability to secure capital, which HuStream had little experience with. Its business model had thus far been based on customer revenue and required only small investments from the founders.

Within HuStream's services-based model, most processes involved in reaching the final product were performed entirely as a service to the customer, and hence were charged to the customer. This business model provided clients with a guided solution through which both the creation process and the end products were well managed and suited to the customers' willingness to pay. In this way, HuStream provided a product through the use of its SDK (software development kit) platform and services. Since

---

[1] *Hustream – Video Production, website landing page, Click on "Video is changing everything" play button, www.hustream.com/, accessed April 10, 2014.*

the co-founders wanted to expand their operations more rapidly, they needed to productize their solution to reach a larger section of the market, which, in turn, would multiply their success exponentially.

To expand and increase revenues, HuStream needed to more effectively manage its operations to serve more clients at one time. Since HuStream was a small company, consisting of seven employees, producing a higher volume of videos would challenge its ability to deliver until it was able to expand. Expansion of a services-based business would require both financial and time commitments. HuStream would need capital investments for personnel in sales, production, customer support, account management, operations, project management and development. There would also be costs related to physical offices and production space. In a market where gaining first-mover advantage was crucial, investing time and money into expansion would hold the business back in terms of its future development. Clients wanted their products developed rapidly; high-calibre clients were unwilling to wait for the construction of a new video production facility, which HuStream might need to build to meet increased demand. But productizing its services-based business model would enable a swift distribution of services over a larger, more diverse range of clientele. How would HuStream balance these forces of building versus executing?

HuStream's overall video output totalled more than 300 videos, which worked out to an average output of 75 videos per year without considering the learning curve faced in the early years, just after the company was founded. Thus, in the future, the average video production would arguably be higher than 75 completed videos per year. Company growth over the past year would be an influencing factor to consider when determining productivity going forward. The overall suggestion was that HuStream should grow steadily.

HuStream's growth in production services, production facilities and highly trained professionals that made the company operate smoothly would increase pressure on maintaining the high quality of account management deliverables. HuStream was committed to delivering exceptional products and services in a timely fashion, which was always a crucial asset to the company; however, in a time crunch, foregoing its commitment to quality would not be an option. HuStream was uncertain whether developing fully productized solutions of products and services as technical advisers urged would replace the need for high-quality account management. The Matejcek's consider account management critical but advisors are offering a different opinion. These two counter-balancing forces need to be considered.

Given HuStream's SDK platform and easy-to-use interface, would the company continue to be able to reach customers who had a less critical need for high-touch account management? Developing this kind of functional interface and platform would take time. HuStream's management and development team estimated the creation of this leading-edge platform and interface would take three years. The user experience would provide a unique competitive advantage, by enabling clients to feel as if they were having an intimate one-on-one relationship with the website. As Lawrence and her team analyzed the current situation, they looked at HuStream's current business offerings and contemplated the most plausible approaches to manage the shift in business that could bring the company greater financial success.

MANAGEMENT TEAM

HuStream employed seven people in various management roles and responsibilities. Peter and Amy Matejcek had co-founded the business in October 2008, as a producer of content for educational training. They had grown the company to its current state and knew it well. Peter Matejcek held the CEO position and was responsible for sales, business development and the office setup. He lead all sales efforts and realized his limited capacity for the multiple roles but he did them better than anyone they had tried in these positions. Amy Matejcek held the COO position and brought her deep skills in content creation, marketing and account management.

HuStream was a lean company with a few key employees, starting with Jon, the developer and tech support; Reid in client services; and the creative team led by Jordy and his sub-team. Marketing responsibilities were contracted out to local marketing firms. The company had recently spent $10,000[2] on a marketing strategy, but it had not successfully convert viewers to new customers.

Their headquarters situated in Kelowna, BC, Canada, held and offices were set up in several Canadian cities to service customers across Canada and the United States. HuStream's video production process streamlined customers' videos and made them flexible to align with their marketing and goals. This process started with Scope and Discovery, which identified the customer's needs, goals, timing and budget, and progressed to the Shoot and Post Production steps, which ensured top-class editing, visuals and graphics. Finally the process maximized traffic to the video through an effective launch strategy. The founders recognized that they lacked a production team to produce material and content for the videos, although they had good contacts and relationships with people in local markets who produced good-quality content and videos, and who were readily available under contract in the future.

DEVELOPMENT AND NEW ARCHITECTURE

Technology development, conducted by Jon, HuStream's lone developer, was built using an architecture of java, PHP (PHP: Hypertext Preprocessor), HTML (HyperText Markup Language), Windows-based servers and secured with SSL encryption for account and password security. The SDK platform that customers purchased for their own use created a toolkit, which could be resold to give clients the ability to edit their own content and create interactive pages in a secure environment. Although the technical people urged HuStream to build out this capability quickly, the Matejceks were uncertain how their custom-tailored services were consistent with that kind of productized toolkit. The toolkit operated through a web-based browser providing cloud-platform access from anywhere in the world.

In addition to the development platform, Jon, the developer, chose web services as a foundational technology. Web services architecture was a technology that created dynamic systems-based business models around usable and adaptable user experiences. This technology, which provided interoperable digital objects, such as streaming video, had grown and developed over the past few years, and ensured HuStream had a strong foundation for its technology development processes. Recently, experts had promoted the use of standardized back ends and flexible front ends for architectures and business models.[3] The web services architecture described the principles for creating dynamic, loosely coupled systems based on services that could be delivered on multiple platforms.

BUSINESS CRITERIA

The business criteria for HuStream's success included the typical business model metrics of profitability, increasing sales, creating a unique value proposition for customers, reducing the budget and creating

---

[2] All currency amounts are shown in Canadian dollars unless otherwise indicated.
[3] Henry Chesbrough, *Open Services Innovation: Rethinking Your Business to Grow and Compete in a New Era*, Jossey-Bass, A Wiley Imprint, San Francisco, 2011, Figure 2.1.

sound management structure. The Matejcek's had also identified several unique criteria for success based on their experiences with prior customers: lots of video content, a competitive industry, the need to be on the leading edge and the need to interact with people. These critical criteria had led to customers who were ready to pay for interactive content and platform tools.

STRATEGIC BALANCE

HuStream had developed its services-based business model over many years and had recently engaged technology experts who suggested the company make its business models into more of a products-based model, which might be turned out in mass scale with little customization. The Matejceks considered how "productization" would work and how to balance this new model with their historical competitive advantage, which had been built by creating customized services-based videos. Amy Matejcek hesitated to leave this lucrative customization segment but wanted to balance it with the idea of creating packages of products, solutions and services that could complement HuStream's existing customized products. How would the company's new strategy adjust to reflect this balance among products, solutions and services in the right combination? And what would change in the strategic balance going forward?

INDUSTRIES

In addition to balancing the roadmap of products and services, the HuStream co-founders needed to consider which industries would make a good fit for its offerings and, consequently, how profitable those industries would be.

Interactive content seemed to be the next big development in online video where video "producers can build direct relationships with their customers" (slide 40) [4] bypassing existing channels and creating new markets. In addition, the video game market represents a US$93 billion market in 2013, according to Gartner Research[5] to which HuStream's interactive buttons could offer customized user experiences for messaging to users. Given that Internet users were drawn to interactive features, this influence caught the eye of many big-name companies, such as Microsoft, Intel and Lenovo, along with more than 40 other customers. Using interactive material gave customers a competitive edge that could benefit their products' appeal and propel HuStream's customers' business overall.

Lawrence arrived at the office on Wednesday morning and prepared to meet her team to discuss potential vertical opportunities that HuStream could take advantage of. Given this company's untapped market potential, the team had already decided that HuStream's pressing issue was to develop a sustainable business model to encourage the growth of the company. In anticipation of the meeting, Lawrence had prepared some analyses of industries that HuStream could potentially enter.

Lawrence's team knew numerous potential solutions could lead to HuStream's success; however, Peter Matejcek could focus on only a few potential industries for sales and business development. He was a good salesperson but he could work on these areas for only so many hours in the day, as he also needed to cover all his other many roles and responsibilities. As a result, Lawrence and her team would need to identify the three best industries.

---

[4] Mark Suster, "Building an Internet Based Video Company," @msuster, upfront resources, September 2013, www.slideshare.net/msuster/online-video-market-sept-2013, accessed April 10, 2014.
[5] Gartner, Inc., "Gartner Says Worldwide Video Game Market to Total $93 Billion in 2013," press release, October 29, 2013, www.gartner.com/newsroom/id/2614915, accessed March 30, 2014.

Lawrence met with her team to discuss potential ideas for industries that would give HuStream the greatest ability for increasing revenue generation. Which distribution channel and marketing strategy could best complement these industry choices for the fastest success rate? Which of these industries would respond best to productized or services-based solutions? Lawrence and her team created an extensive list of potential markets to generate increased profits, including entertainment, instructional videos, tourism, sports media, recruiting, education, retail, automobile (either repairs or retail) and many others.

Entertainment

A particular vertical of interest to Lawrence and her consulting team was the entertainment industry. As a result of the North American public's excessive interest in popular culture, an immense untapped market existed for producing entertainment- and information-based online video content. Media outlets such as CTV (Canadian Television), CBC (Canadian Broadcasting Corporation), Rogers and Global had been providing a constant stream of online content to their viewers long before the larger boom of online Internet content. Through discussions and market research, the consulting team returned to the potential for interactive video in the entertainment industry.

The entertainment industry had undergone many changes since the early 2000s. The team noted that, in terms of detailed content, users of media sites had high demands, which were increasing quickly. Broadly speaking, the onset of these changes had begun with the DVD industry, which had quickly expanded video content in the entertainment industry by providing people around the world with affordable, digital-quality movies and television shows.[6] Experts in the entertainment industry reported that this trend was the beginning of increased expectations around entertainment products and services.

When streaming technology was introduced in 2007, a major pivot occurred in the presentation of entertainment content. "Streaming really exploded around the year 2010," commented Adam Leipzig, a media specialist. "We shifted from a commodity economy of entertainment, where we had to own CDs, DVDs and so on, into a pure experience economy."[7] This shift created a bridge between television and the Internet, providing viewers with an array of online content at their fingertips. The pivot shifted from product-based markets where consumers owned CDs, DVDs and the hardware to play them, to a services-based market where the content and players were embedded in laptops, desktops and mobile devices. Web services architecture was poised to have a profound effect on the entertainment industry and its supporting platforms. W3C, the leading worldwide Internet consortium and founder of the URL (uniform resource locator) addressing system, promoted the ability of these foundational web services capabilities and platforms to give rise to new web-based business models wrapping varying combinations into products and services to satisfy customers' needs.[8]

As a result of viewers shifting their consumption patterns, online content exposure powered by web services seemed to be a foundational platform. As the team thought it through, viewers could access an array of constant online content, such as television, movies, sports and news. The way that a business framed its delivery of online content could maintain or gain a competitive edge since customers required a balance of visually pleasing elements and technical functionality. At this time, these digital landscapes held increasingly influential roles in the success of a business. Because of HuStream's ability to create

[6] Paul Sawers, "How Technology Is Changing the Entertainment Industry, According to Adam Leipzig," blog post, September 19, 2013, http://thenextweb.com/insider/2013/09/19/adam-leipzig/#!y19gz, accessed March 30, 2014.
[7] Ibid.
[8] W3C, "Web Services Architecture: W3C Working Group Note 11 February 2004, February 11, 2004, http://www.w3.org/TR/ws-arch/, accessed March 30, 2014.

interactive content for an array of business concepts, the consulting team clearly identified that one of the potentially best industries for HuStream would be creating interactive shows and media content.

Suppose viewers could go to a web-based platform and receive updates directly from their favourite characters or the show of their choice? Lawrence's team considered this possibility, as many people would likely be drawn to such content. Viewers would feel as though they were receiving a first-hand, customized experience with each click, which would reduce the perceived distance between themselves and their favourite celebrities.

As an example, such popular CTV shows as *Big Bang Theory* and *Big Brother Canada* could produce video and website clips that used interactive buttons to offer alternative viewing experiences and additional products for sale. "Dim the lights, hook up your player to a 50″ TV with surround sound, and you could at least get close to pretending you were enjoying a theatrical experience."[9] Imagine that experience with added HuStream interactive content and toolkits through which shows could be perused.

Another program that could benefit from interactive content was *Hockey Night in Canada*. As Peter Matejcek mused aloud, "I know my boys love hockey and having their favourite player talk directly to them would be a huge selling point for them." Marshal Redrick, a marketing expert on Lawrence's team, expressed interest in hockey and how interactive content directed toward dedicated fans might have a substantial impact on consumers in this area.[10] *Hockey Night in Canada*, owned by CBC, was the longest running television broadcasting program in Canadian history. Considering the dense market of hockey fans in Canada, which was greater than in any other country in the world, Redrick argued that this avenue might generate major revenue for HuStream.

However, the broadcasting industry could change dramatically over the next few years. In fact, CBC had recently lost its rights to hockey broadcasting in Canada to Rogers TV, a broadcasting giant in its own right, which, for $5.2 billion had landed a 12-year contract for exclusive TV and digital rights to broadcast all Canadian national hockey games, including the national hockey league (NHL). Avid hockey viewers from across Canada were shocked at the possible loss of the beloved CBC broadcast of *Hockey Night in Canada*.

Even NHL commissioner Gary Bettman recognized the need for collaboration to deliver content to viewers through varying avenues: "We wanted a relationship where we and our partner would have the flexibility to move among platforms because people, particularly of varying ages, are consuming their entertainment differently than they ever did before and differently by age."[11] As technologies developed, the league "may be looking at things in the course of this deal that don't currently exist," Bettman continued. Viewers, likely paying for the extra privilege, would be able to access specific content on the devices of their choosing.

No one was certain what the media industry would look like within the next few years but these changes in hockey broadcasting resonated well with HuStream's business offerings and suggested that interactive content might be a major influence on broadcasting; however, the Matejceks were not well experienced with gaining access to these types of large broadcast customers.

---

[9] Paul Sawers, "How Technology Is Changing the Entertainment Industry, According to Adam Leipzig," blog post, September 19, 2013, http://thenextweb.com/insider/2013/09/19/adam-leipzig/#!y19gz, accessed March 30, 2014.
[10] Simon Houpt, "A New Chapter for Iconic Brand Hockey Night in Canada," Globe and Mail, November 26, 2013, www.theglobeandmail.com/news/national/a-new-chapter-for-iconic-brand-hockey-night-in-canada/article15625191/, accessed March 30, 2014.
[11] Ibid.

Do-It-Yourself (DIY)

As the team explored other options and analyzed global industry trends regarding market share and market size, team member Lily Newman, who had some experience in hotel maintenance, raised the potential use of videos for repair advice.

The multibillion-dollar do-it-yourself (DIY) industry had seen steady growth in the past few years. Recession-driven financial caution had given rise to the global DIY culture along with the widespread availability of easy-to-install products that required some assembly. Currently worth US$678 billion, the global DIY industry was expected to continue to grow to be worth US$716.2 billion by 2015.[12] The rapidly increasing number of products and services, including websites, television programs, books and tools focused specifically on optimizing DIY tasks, was on the rise, fuelling the growth of the industry and the potential for development of interactive video content. The DIY industry provided a multitude of existing content, which would reduce the necessary capital investment for HuStream. A significant factor that resonated within the market was the home improvement segment of DIY.

The home improvement segment alone contributed significantly to the DIY industry overall. With major players in Canada such as RONA, Home Hardware, Canadian Tire and Home Depot, the expansion options into this market were huge. Cost-wary individuals were spending their time and money to improve the value of their home and property to maintain their commercial value. As a result, they were increasing their use of DIY tools and mechanisms, which had led to noticeable growth in the DIY market and could provide a niche for HuStream to satisfy.

Education

The education industry had proved to be HuStream's most responsive and lucrative industry. The company had secured 10 universities and colleges as some of their first customers and had continued to generate sales leads every day. In fact, Peter Matejcek had lined up the University of Michigan for a sales call later that day, after a meeting with the consulting teams.

The educational institutions already had video content and often had their own internal television and radio studio production capabilities. As well, these postsecondary schools were communicating with potential students who sought interactive conversations with admissions staff and were eager to have virtual tours. Current and soon to be graduating students also needed to differentiate themselves from other students with experience that would stand out on their résumés, perhaps by using interactive content button which others would not have. The education sector seemed to represent a ripe and rewarding industry for HuStream.

Using HuStream's capabilities, schools' existing video content could be shaped into interactive content, which would create a competitive advantage differentiating these schools from others that provided traditional video and written content. Moving to interactive content could increase traffic to an institution's website, which would in turn increase the positive image of the school and ultimately increase enrollment. Students selected schools based on numerous factors, including the school's distance from home and its scholarships, prestige, image and support network. The support network of a school undoubtedly included the administration and faculty; yet, the school's website was also a secondary

---

[12] *Global Industry Analysts, Inc., "Global Market for DIY and Home Improvement to Reach US$716.2 Billion by 2015, According to New Report by Global Industry Analysts, Inc.," press release, PRWeb Online Visibility from Vocus, January 30, 2012, www.prweb.com/releases/do_it_yourself_DIY/home_improvement_products/prweb9136735.htm, accessed March 30, 2014.*

consideration. The school's website included supporting tools to help students find the information they were searching for, but poorly designed and complex websites could frustrate and discourage new and potential students. Interactive content on a services-based platform could increase the conversion from traffic to new customers.

Universities, colleges and other institutions almost always had existing video content, which reduced the capital investment required to produce high-quality content. They would also not require in-house production facilities to be provided by HuStream, as their current content and campus infrastructure could be used to satisfy this need.

Other

Among the many other industries considered by the consulting team were automotive, hospitality and tourism, real estate, advertising, landscaping, athletics and sports, oil and gas, employee training, weddings, computer software, casinos, online dating and other generic marketing and training activities, including vlogging (video blogging) and online tutorials. Driven by factors similar to the DIY segment, the automotive industry generated considerable demands for solutions for both customers and manufacturers. Customers were interested in automotive repair, maintenance and improvement, whereas manufacturers were interested in solutions for automotive advertising, sales, manuals and maintenance. This market would continue to generate demand for solutions because of such supporting factors as increases in the global number of cars on the road, the longer average life of vehicles and the general wear and tear of parts and accessories.

Lawn, garden and landscaping also provided lucrative opportunities for interactive solutions. Homeowners and small business owners were always looking for ways to stretch every dollar, including by reducing their dependence on professional landscaping services.

Hospitality and tourism provided an abundance of avenues. The needs in this segment included features directed toward municipalities and their marketing strategies to promote their cities. This segment could also be directed toward travel agencies, such as Expedia and their online service models. Cruise ship promotion was also considered because a personal virtual tour could be offered through interactive video.

Other generic uses not defined to a specific industry included a wide range of marketing and training activities. Advertising and marketing agencies could also use interactive videos as a tool to help their customers improve their marketing and promotion efforts by providing them with a competitive advantage.

PARTNERS

As Lawrence considered what the Matejceks would do, she realized they needed partners for this business to be successful. But what partners would have the best fit, and at what points would they be integrate into HuStream's business model? The systems thinking community was promoting the use of ecosystems for collaborators, partners, third-party content and other providers necessary for the installation and implementation of technology.[13] Balancing the services-based and the product-based company proved a

---

[13] Henry Chesbrough, *Open Services Innovation: Rethinking Your Business to Grow and Compete in a New Era*, Jossey-Bass, A Wiley Imprint, San Francisco, 2011, Chapter 2, Figure 2.2 Open Services Value Chain, p. 35.

difficult task. The problem was there was no predetermined process for creating the balance that HuStream needed.

BUSINESS MODEL

Lawrence began to contemplate how to generate revenue through the entertainment option. Of all the options the team had explored, it had considered only the most potentially lucrative industries. In the entertainment segment, the pricing strategy would be based on a per-episode fee and any additional maintenance fees that may apply.

When considering the DIY segment, the team proposed a per video profit model. As with the entertainment option, the prices at increasing volumes would be negotiated downward. The team considered the various types of DIY videos. Education appeared to be a very lucrative industry, and some schools might be price-insensitive, such that HuStream could consider how to detect price flexibility.

HuStream's customers generally wanted affordable solutions, which required an operational budget that was as tight as possible. With these new industries, the profitability potential would grow, and Lawrence's team needed to propose the business model profitability to the Matejceks. Funding for any major initiatives would also need to be considered.

DECISIONS

As Lawrence sat contemplating the recommendations her team would make, she considered which industries were the best options, and how the Matejceks would make money by scaling this business. Lawrence and her team needed to present clear value propositions for both customers and users within these industries, such that the Matejceks could articulate the strength of their tools and services to their potential customers. Lawrence's team would need to identify additional personnel, architecture changes and functionality that they might need and how those costs would impact the budget. The outlook seemed to be a combination of products and services development; just productizing would not likely meet what the Matejceks had in mind, so they needed to carefully consider how much of each type of work they did. Clearly, the user experience in each of these areas would be an important part of that decision.

H A R V A R D | B U S I N E S S | S C H O O L

BRIEF CASES

9-914-537
JANUARY 8, 2014

JOHN QUELCH

ALISA ZALOSH

CleanSpritz

Claire Beaton watched her colleagues tidy their desks and shut down their computers as, one by one, they departed for the weekend. It was Friday afternoon, September 21, 2012, but Beaton, brand manager for CleanSpritz all-purpose cleaning spray, knew that this would not be a weekend of rest and relaxation. On Monday morning, Beaton was to lead a marketing strategy session with Steve Logan, senior vice president of strategy for MJ Brenner's household cleaning division, and selected members of Logan's advisory team. Convinced that a concentrated version of the historically popular CleanSpritz cleaner was the best way to slow its continuing sales decline, Logan had given Beaton six months to research and plan a concentrate launch strategy. He was eager to hear her recommendation.

Beaton knew as well as anyone that CleanSpritz's future was uncertain. For five consecutive years, the company's annual sales had declined at an average rate of 7.5% as some long-loyal customers tried environmentally friendlier substitutes, while others sought cheaper options. Under pressure to refresh a stale brand image, CleanSpritz altered its existing all-purpose spray formula in 2009; the new formula reduced chemical content by 15% and was more biodegradable than the original formula. Relative to "greener" competitors, though, CleanSpritz's formula and packaging fared poorly.

Also in 2009, CleanSpritz launched without much fanfare a 3:1 concentrated version of its all-purpose spray. Consumer demand for cleaning concentrates was climbing, and CleanSpritz hoped to gain first-mover advantage in what they believed was an emerging market of consumers seeking to minimize both packaging waste and carbon footprints. Despite these changes, CleanSpritz revenues continued to drop. MJ Brenner's household products executives questioned the brand's relevance. Was the CleanSpritz brand, widely recognized for decades, becoming a liability precisely because it was associated with a time when environmental issues were not a priority?

In February 2012, MJ Brenner and CleanSpritz managers had gathered to discuss the product's future. The meeting was heated; MJ Brenner executives felt that CleanSpritz was draining financial resources that could be used to fuel other growing branches of the large consumer products company and suggested reducing CleanSpritz distribution. CleanSpritz managers disagreed; they felt their concentrate was a worthy competitor in a market ready to take off. What they needed, they said, was six months to test marketing concepts. Heavy promotion of the concentrate, or perhaps a stronger version of the concentrate designed specifically to refill CleanSpritz 32 oz. spray containers, along with consumer education on the concentrate's benefits, could reverse the declining sales trend. They convinced Logan and his team to reconvene on September 24 when the CleanSpritz team, led by Beaton, would recommend a strategic plan.

Beaton stared at the whiteboard in her office, which outlined four distinct paths the concentrate's future could take, as shown in **Table 1**. Making the right recommendation at Monday's meeting would be critical for CleanSpritz, as well as her own future with MJ Brenner.

Table 1 CleanSpritz Concentrate Strategic Options

Option 1 Concentrate Re-launch	Option 2A Refill Pouch	Option 2B Refill Dissolvable Packet	Base Case/ Status Quo
Re-launch existing 3:1 concentrate with heavy promotion focused on environmental benefits	Add to product line a stronger, 4:1 concentrate in a lightweight, recyclable pouch for 32 oz. bottle refill	Add to product line a stronger, 4:1 concentrate in an innovative dissolvable packet for 32 oz. bottle refill	Make no changes in short term. Consider re-launching with 99% biodegradable spray (2 years) or cartridge system (12 months)

MJ Brenner

MJ Brenner: Company Background

MJ Brenner was founded in 1925 in Toledo, Ohio, by Michael John Brenner. Originally a paint manufacturer, the company expanded beyond paints to include products for paint preparation and clean-up. In 1950, the company developed products for both industrial and household cleaners. By 1975, the company was producing two industry-leading products: (1) WinWipe, a household window cleaner, and (2) Floormax, an industrial floor cleaner. The 1980s marked a period of continued growth in the cleaning industry through acquisition and international distribution.

MJ Brenner's 2011 revenues totaled $6.2 billion, with 80% of sales coming from the U.S. In the U.S., sales were generated by the following divisions within MJ Brenner:

- Household Cleaning Products: 31.5%
- Industrial Cleaning Products: 40%
- Auto Cleaning Products: 28.5%

High-quality, strong branding and innovation were hallmarks of MJ Brenner's family of consumer products. The company invested 7% of sales in research and development to ensure products exceeded customer expectations and competitive offerings. Branding was a critical component of MJ Brenner's consumer-goods marketing strategy. Each brand had its own brand team; the company spent 25% of a brand's revenues annually on marketing to grow and reinforce brand awareness. The company rarely made changes to products, logos, or packaging for established brands.

MJ Brenner: Organization

In 2012, MJ Brenner remained a private company with roughly two-thirds of the ownership shared by Brenner's descendants, and the remaining third by employees and a select group of private investors. The company employed more than 10,000 employees worldwide, and manufactured and distributed more than 30 products under 11 distinct brands. Products fell into three distinct categories: industrial cleaning products, household cleaning products, and auto cleaning products; see **Table 2**.

Table 2 MJ Brenner Products and Brands by Division

Industrial Products	Home Cleaning Products	Auto Cleaning Products
• Carpet stain removers • Industrial floor cleaner • Floor polish • Wall and surface cleaner • Concrete cleaner/stain remover	• Countertop sprays • Window cleaners • Disinfecting wipes • Toilet cleaners • Tile cleaners • Floor cleaners • Dish detergents	• Cleaning wipes • Leather cleaner • Freshener • Exterior polish
Brands: MJCleaner, StainLift	Brands: WinWipe, CleanSpritz, BubbleScrub, TileSmile, GrimeBust, SparKleen	Brands: AutoNew, Longleather, BrightBurst

Each of the three divisions was run independently; each had a division leadership team and division departments for sales, finance, manufacturing, distribution, operations, and market research functions. Each brand within a division's brand portfolio had its own brand team responsible for marketing, brand, and product development strategies for each product. Branding teams consisted of a brand manager, an assistant brand manager, and between one and three coordinators. The branding teams collaborated with departments within their division to support their strategic efforts.

U.S. Household Cleaning Industry

U.S. Household Cleaning Market Size

U.S. sales of all household cleaning products—including cleaning solutions and tools for hard surfaces, rugs, furniture, and floors—totaled $5.04 billion in 2010. Hard-surface cleaners represented 56% of household cleaning sales and generated $1.46 billion in revenue in 2010. (The next largest segment, cleaners and deodorizers for rugs and fabrics, represented just 13.5% of total 2010 industry sales.) Hard-surface cleaners included, among others, all-purpose cleaning sprays, tub and toilet cleaners, window and appliance cleaners, and products to unclog drains.

All-purpose Cleaning Sprays 2011

All-purpose cleaners came primarily in spray and wipe form. Designed to rid dirt and grime from kitchen and bath counters, these products left a satisfying scent that homemakers associated with a clean home. Sales for all-purpose cleaners in the U.S. totaled $384 million in 2011.

Trends

The economic recession that began in 2008 in the U.S. impacted the market for household cleaning products and, more specifically, hard surface cleaners. In 2006, U.S. sales for hard-surface cleaners sold at food, drug and mass merchants *excluding* WalMart (a measure known as FDMx) totaled $1.64

billion, but by 2010 that FDMx figure had dropped by 11% to $1.46 billion.[1] Not only were consumers more price sensitive as a result of the economic downturn, but their cleaning habits had changed as well. To conserve resources, consumers used fewer cleaning products, and replenished those products at a slower rate than they had before the recession. Despite a slight rise in 2011 consumer confidence which boosted usage rates slightly in 2011, forecasted FDMx sales for hard-surface cleaners predicted a continuing sales decline with just $1.3 billion in 2015.[2] See **Table 3** for usage trends.

Table 3 All-purpose Cleaner Usage Trends, 2009–2011*

	2009	2010	2011
Percent of population using diluted spray cleaner	79%	79%	79%
Number of uses per month	99	94	104
Number of 32 oz bottles used per year	4.75	4.5	5

* Figures loosely based on Mintel Report: Household Cleaning, The Consumer, May 2011.

Environmental concerns

Consumers have long wondered about the impact of everyday chemical products on health and the environment. By 2000, the increasingly powerful voices of consumer and environmental advocacy groups helped to make environmental issues a priority for corporations across industries in the U.S. and abroad. With respect to cleaning products, consumers worried about the potential harm posed by household cleaning products in the short and long term. Frequently asked questions included:

- What are the consequences of repeated skin exposure to cleaning fluids?
- Are children at risk if cleaning residue is ingested along with food?
- What are the long-term effects of using non-biodegradable products on our water and food supply?
- Will repeated exposure to household chemicals disrupt hormones or cause cancer?

Demand for "green" products—meaning less chemically invasive and more environmentally friendly—grew across industries during the early 2000s, from food to beauty products to clothing and cleaning agents. In 2006, just 17 new products in the household cleaning industry made "environmentally friendly product" their key message on packaging. In 2010, that figure increased more than nine-fold to 164.[3]

All-purpose Surface Cleaners: 2011 Competitive Environment

The five largest consumer products companies produced the eight leading all-purpose cleaning brands and generated 79% of U.S. all-purpose cleaner sales. These companies battled for market share; because there was little product differentiation among products, consumers were very responsive to price. Promotions and price wars were frequent and fierce. See **Table 4** for 2011 market share for all-purpose surface cleaners, and **Table 5** for indexed costs and pricing for the five market leaders.

---

[1] Mintel Report: Household Cleaning: The Market - US - June 2011.

[2] Mintel Report: Household Cleaning: The Market - US - June 2011.

[3] Mintel Report: Household Cleaning: The Market - US - June 2011.

Table 4 2011 Market Share for All-purpose Cleaners

Parent Company	Brand	Market Share
Linseer	Shinee	13%
	KleenUP	6%
Onidum	Glisten	11%
	123 Clean	8%
MJ Brenner	CleanSpritz	14%
	WinWipe	2%
MagicCS	Magic Mary	14%
Randsee	Clear n Clean	11%
	Other	14%
	Private label	7%
	Total	100%

Note: Linseer, Onidum, and MJ Brenner each produced two leading all-purpose cleaning brands. Magic CS and Randsee produced one all-purpose cleaner each.

Table 5 Indexed Costs and Pricing for Leading All-purpose Cleaners (per Unit)

Brand Name	CleanSpritz	Shinee	Glisten	Magic Mary	Clear n Clean
Packaging	100	104	105	105	103
Chemicals	100	87	94	98	101
Media	100	108	88	101	95
Total costs	100	99	87	104	99
Recommended retail price	100	88	87	103	105

Note: Figures in **Table 5** provide costs and pricing for each brand in relation to CleanSpritz. So, for example, while Shinee's packaging costs (104) are 4% higher than CleanSpritz's, its chemicals cost (87) is 13% less than CleanSpritz's (100–87).

Between 2007 and 2011, private labels and small, independent brands of all-purpose cleaners (labeled "other" in **Table 4**, above) experienced the highest revenue gains. Grocery stores, mass merchandisers, and warehouse stores marketed private-label products under their respective retail brands. Private-label products were offered at a lower price than branded cleaners and, as a result, sales of private labels increased during the recession. Fourteen percent of the market (representing $53.8 million) was shared by smaller, independent brands whose differentiating factors included— but were not limited to—environmental friendliness (natural sources, recycled packaging, etc.) and aroma-therapeutic scents.

Distribution

Consumers could purchase all-purpose cleaners at a variety of outlets in 2011. Food, drug, and mass merchant retailers (commonly referred to as "FDM" retailers) accounted for $199.68 million of the $384 million all-purpose cleaning sales in 2011; supermarkets alone accounted for $139.78 million, or 70%, of these sales.[4] Outside of FDM, distribution channels included smaller grocery chains and local markets, convenience stores, home improvement and hardware stores, warehouse clubs, discount and dollar stores, online retailers, and natural food stores.

---

[4] Mintel Report: Household Cleaning: The Market - US - June 2011.

Profit margins at large supermarket chains were small; typical operating margins were somewhere between 2% and 3% before interest and taxes. Volume, therefore, was critical to supermarkets' profitability; and to lure consumers into their stores, supermarkets discounted consumer staples. Known as "loss leaders," these items were offered to consumers at a lower price than the price paid by the retailer to the manufacturer. Retailers regularly employed this tactic with all-purpose cleaners as an advertising strategy.

Only the largest supermarkets and mass merchants offered a thorough assortment of all-purpose cleaning brands in one place. At neighborhood grocery stores or convenience stores, for example, a scarcity of shelf space forced proprietors to select just a small variety of products for display. Labor costs related to unpacking, re-shelving, and re-ordering for each product line were also a consideration for retailers.

Industry Advertising and Promotion

The year 2011 found all-purpose cleaners devoting the largest portion of their advertising budget to trade promotions; examples included in-store displays, free product samples, and sweepstakes. Consumer ad campaigns focused primarily on branding, product attributes, and consumer lifestyles. While television and print ads offered a good way to build brand identity, computers and mobile devices offered a way for brands to connect directly with targeted consumers, whether through keyword search advertisements, social media campaigns, or branded websites and mini-sites. Social media provided low-cost access to consumers, but it presented a risk as well. Negative comments or conversation threads, about the product's packaging, ingredients, or management, for example, could rapidly snowball into a conversation involving thousands of consumers and severely damage a brand's carefully crafted reputation.

Pricing campaigns for all-purpose cleaners most often originated with retailers, who collaborated with manufacturers to develop discounted pricing campaigns that could be used to boost customer traffic to the store.

CleanSpritz History

Product Overview

In 1985, MJ Brenner acquired Stalton & Sons. The Midwestern company manufactured two popular cleaning products: CleanSpritz and SparKleen. With steady brand-building efforts both products gained market share in their respective categories. In 2011, the CleanSpritz product line included (1) its anchor product, CleanSpritz all-purpose surface cleaner spray, and (2) a 3:1 concentrated version of the CleanSpritz all-purpose cleaner. CleanSpritz revenues totaled $53.76 million in 2011. Though CleanSpritz was reluctant to make changes to its original formula for fear of diminishing performance and losing loyal customers, research efforts began in 2010 to increase the biodegradability of the CleanSpritz all-purpose cleaner. A 99% biodegradable version was expected to be ready sometime in 2014.

The CleanSpritz all-purpose cleaner came in a 32 oz. spray bottle that varied only slightly in size, shape, and labeling from the bottle launched 20 years earlier. The composition of the spray in 2011 was 96% water and 4% proprietary mix of chemicals.

CleanSpritz Concentrate

In 2008, prompted by consumer concern related to wasteful packaging and carbon footprints from freight, and by the growing popularity of wholesale clubs, CleanSpritz launched the concentrated version of its surface cleaning spray. The concentrate, sold in a 16 oz. plastic bottle, enabled consumers to recreate the original spray's formula by (1) pouring the entire bottle of concentrate into a half-gallon container, such as an old milk jug; (2) filling the rest of the container with water and shaking to combine; (3) pouring the resulting solution into a spray bottle of their choice; and (4) storing the rest for later use. Seven months of consumer testing preceded the concentrate's launch; there was high interest among professional cleaners, as well as consumers looking to save money and help the environment. Though forecasts projected that concentrate volume could reach 30% of all-purpose cleaning volume within four years, actual 2011 concentrate volume amounted to just 20% of total U.S. CleanSpritz volume. See **Exhibit 1** for CleanSpritz sales volume by store type.

The concentrate had both strengths and weaknesses. It benefited consumers in three primary ways: (1) it was more cost effective; (2) the 16 oz. bottle was compact and easy to carry; and (3) it was better for the environment due to smaller package size and reduced pollution from freight transportation. Customer complaints related to the CleanSpritz concentrate included doubt surrounding the efficacy of the concentrated version, and dissatisfaction with the amount of extra work consumers had to perform—measuring, mixing, pouring, and storing. See **Exhibit 2** for CleanSpritz package sizes and pricing for 2011.

CleanSpritz: Advertising

CleanSpritz allocated more than 70% of its ad budget to trade promotions. The smallest allocation was consumer promotions, which included sweepstakes, coupons and rewards programs; in 2011 CleanSpritz further reduced its consumer promotion budget in order to launch a series of new media campaigns. See **Table 6,** below, for a breakdown of CleanSpritz's advertising budget.

Table 6 CleanSpritz Advertising Budget, 2010–2011

CleanSpritz Ad Budget	Dilute 2010	Dilute 2011	Concentrate 2010	Concentrate 2011
Media	20%	23%	20%	22%
Consumer promotion	3.5%	1%	1%	1%
Trade promotion	76.5%	76%	79%	77%

CleanSpritz: Declining Sales

Between 2006 and 2011, CleanSpritz combined revenue from diluted spray and concentrate declined at an average rate of 7.5% annually. One contributing factor was the economic recession. Consumers cut spending and they tried to squeeze more out of the products they purchased, using less of a product like CleanSpritz and taking longer to replenish their supply. In addition, some customers migrated to new, greener alternatives due to concern over standard chemical ingredients, and stronger competition from inexpensive private labels led to sharp price-cutting wars between branded manufacturers.

CleanSpritz's Future: Strategic Options

Beaton reviewed the market research in front of her. Clearly natural product sources and environmentally safe packaging were of interest to consumers. Focus groups conducted by

CleanSpritz in 2010 indicated that 70% consumers, after being educated on the topic, were open to trying concentrates to cut down on packaging for environmental reasons. See **Exhibit 3** for consumer usage study results. Yet, to date, consumer interest had not translated into high sales levels of the CleanSpritz concentrate. This behavioral pattern mirrored a broader trend in U.S. consumers: Actual sales of green household cleaning supplies lagged far behind reported consumer interest in green (and usually higher priced) cleaning supplies. The data confounded researchers and marketers across the industry as they tried to determine the source of consumers' hesitation—was it price? Doubt about the effectiveness of "green" cleaners? Brand confusion? In 2011, sales of green household cleaning supplies represented just 3% of all FDM household cleaning supply sales.[5] By 2011, Claire Beaton and her team were wondering if broad swaths of consumers would be willing to change their behavior in the years ahead—by adding water to concentrate—to benefit the environment.

Beaton pondered this question as she reviewed the two strategic options that she and her brand management team had created over the last two months.

- **Option 1:** Re-launch the existing 3:1 CleanSpritz concentrate.

  This strategy involved heavily promoting the environmental benefits of the existing 3:1 concentrate:

  - Reduced packaging (45% less packaging volume than diluted spray)
  - Less pollution from freight
  - Reuse of old spray bottle

  A 6% increase in ad spending over 2011 could be secured and reallocated so that 60% and 40% of media spending went to the diluted spray and concentrate, respectively. Beaton estimated that this effort would increase 16 oz. concentrate sales by more than 5M Standard Units.[6]

  The greatest risk to this strategy's success was the level at which the concentrate's sales would cannibalize the diluted spray's sales. Beaton projected that 43% of new concentrate SUs would come at the expense of lost diluted spray sales. MJ Brenner's finance team, however, projected the rate of cannibalization would be significantly higher, closer to 55%.

- **Option 2:** Add to existing product line a stronger, 4:1 concentrate designed specifically to refill an existing 32 oz. (ideally CleanSpritz) spray bottle, to be packaged in either a lightweight pouch or a dissolvable packet.

  With environmental benefits in mind, packaging designers recommended two environmentally friendly, innovative package designs for the 4:1 refill concentrate:

  - 6.4 oz. lightweight, 100% recyclable pouch

  Consumers would need scissors to snip a dotted line across a corner of the pouch. Then, consumers would pour all of the concentrate into the mouth of an old 32 oz. spray bottle and fill to the top with water to create the CleanSpritz dilute.

  - 6.4 oz. water soluble packet

---

[5] Mintel Market 2011.

[6] A standard unit, or SU, represents a standardized measure that enables comparison of products on the basis of an equal number of uses. In this case, one SU equals 100 uses.

This clear packet resembled plastic but was made of 100% biodegradable materials. The packet, when exposed to water, dissolved completely. Consumers would need only to drop the tubular-shaped packet through the mouth of an old 32 oz. spray bottle and fill the rest with water. The packet itself and the solution inside the packet would mix with water to form the CleanSpritz dilute.

4:1 Refill Concentrate: Benefits: Both of these refill package options presented CleanSpritz with a strong platform for marketing; both the concentrate itself and its packaging made for compelling advertising messages that supported CleanSpritz's commitment to the environment. Would former CleanSpritz customers abandon their newfound green or private-label products and return to the CleanSpritz brand once its commitment to the environment was advertised?

4:1 Refill Concentrate: Risks: Unlike the 3:1 concentrate, neither package could be manufactured internally. Two smaller subcontractors would supply the packaging; this meant that product quality and on-time delivery were outside of Beaton's control. Beaton also worried about the contractors' ability to meet capacity demands, as neither had ever produced packages in the numbers that would be required by CleanSpritz. Additionally, initial start-up investment would elevate 4:1 refill concentrate costs by 41% and 33% for the packet and pouch, respectively, for the first million SUs produced.

See **Exhibit 4** for results from an August 2012 consumer evaluation of packaging options.

Beaton was concerned by the discrepancy between reported consumer interest in green alternatives, and actual sales. Though 2011 consumer confidence was higher, would that translate to increased sales or would consumers stick with less expensive private labels? Beaton and her team had decided the refill package's retail price should be $5.69.

Distribution was a concern as well. Retailers relied on CleanSpritz diluted spray, and other all-purpose cleaners, to draw customers to their stores—though usually at a loss. Why should they be willing to reduce shelf space for the existing spray products to make room for concentrates?

Comparative Analysis: Recyclable Pouch versus Dissolvable Packet

Beaton's whiteboard highlighted the key differences between the pouch and the packet, in relation to each other as well as the existing 3:1 concentrate.

4:1 Refill Pouch	4:1 Refill Dissolvable Packet
1. 14% cost savings (vs. diluted spray) in packaging and delivery	1. 6% cost savings in packaging and delivery
2. Packaging materials volume reduced 85%	2. Packaging materials volume reduced 90%
3. Consumer familiarity with pouch across food and beverage industries for 20 years, increasing adoption in cleaning industry.	3. Consumer unfamiliarity would mandate consumer communication plan; consumer concern/doubt related to 100% dissolution of packaging
4. 100% recyclable	4. New, groundbreaking packaging option for liquid agent; previously used for magazine and newspaper containment; only 2 other liquid clients to date
5. Firm, rigid base design enables easy stand-alone display on shelves	
6. Can be shipped in existing shipping containers used for 3:1 concentrate	5. Wobbly when standing alone; display would require shipping container that could be opened and used as shelf display with slots to hold packets upright
7. Less sturdy than plastic 3:1 bottle	
a. More leaks during transport	
b. More likely to burst or rip if dropped	

8. Messier than 3:1 plastic bottle
  a. Requires scissors to cut spout; if not cut on dotted line, some spillage likely
  b. More challenging to aim spout directly into spray bottle than pouring plastic 3:1 bottle into half gallon container
	6. Very easy to use; slides through standard opening of 32 oz. spray bottle; no mess if used properly
	7. Less sturdy than pouch and plastic bottle
	  a. Greater chance of leaking during transport
	  b. Most likely to burst or rip if dropped or snagged

Production Costs: The recycled pouch would produce cost savings of 14% when compared to the diluted spray, due to fewer materials and reduced shipping costs. The dissolvable packet's cost savings amounted to 6% annually. Most of the packet's savings came from reduced shipping costs; CleanSpritz, as an early adopter of the packet, would pay a premium. See **Exhibit 5** for a cost breakdown of proposed and existing product lines.

Pricing: See **Exhibit 6** for manufacturer and retail prices for the proposed and existing product lines. Concentrate prices would have to be low enough to compel loyal diluted spray users to switch to concentrate.

Volume Forecasts: Volume forecasts of CleanSpritz's branding team were far more optimistic than those produced by the division's finance department. Beaton, who was present during focus group research sessions and very familiar with third-party consumer research studies related to cleaning and consumer behavior, felt strongly that consumers would be willing to both increase spending and change their behavior in 2013. The finance department, on the other hand, assumed consumers across the U.S. would continue to rein in spending. Finance also believed that nearly all (80%) of concentrate sales would come at the expense of the diluted spray. Both Beaton and the finance department projected that cannibalization would primarily affect the diluted spray and not the 3:1 concentrate.[7]

	Projected 4:1 Concentrate Standard Units (SUs)	Cannibalization Rate (of diluted spray)
CleanSpritz brand team	6,195,757	60%
Division finance team	3,097,878	80%

Promotion and Advertising for 4:1 concentrate: Beaton and the brand team proposed a 6.5% increase over the 2010 advertising and promotion budget. Consumer advertising for the 4:1 concentrate would focus on green themes and ease of use. Sales collateral to entice retailers to stock the concentrate would focus on retailer cost reductions, most importantly (1) product storage requirements (65% less), (2) transportation costs (70% less), and (3) handling (65% less), rather than the existing diluted spray and concentrate product lines. Beaton also felt that retailers would not ignore the concentrate's ability to deliver 9% profit margins—especially as CleanSpritz diluted spray was a standard loss-leader for supermarket ad campaigns.

---

[7] This assumption was based on (1) focus groups of loyal 3:1 users who, surprisingly, exhibited reluctance to switch to a new concentrate product, and (2) future advertising campaigns that would target dilute users and not existing concentrate users.

Conclusion

As she mulled over her options, Beaton glanced at her computer and noticed two unread emails. The first was from Anne Foley, the division's social media manager, entitled "Messaging problem." Beaton clicked on the email:

Claire,

Thanks for meeting with me yesterday to explain the concentrate push and your proposed advertising strategies. I have to be honest here. Examples of false advertising spread like wildfire online, and I'm worried about touting the environmental benefits of the concentrate and its packaging when the product itself contains non-biodegradable ingredients. In addition, the U.S. Government is still working on labeling standards and it's likely that the language you use in the short term regarding environmental friendliness will have to be changed once federal guidelines for green labeling are firmly in place.

I'll be available over the weekend should you want to discuss alternative strategies. Perhaps we could think about creating a new brand for the concentrate, and focus messaging on novel packaging rather than environmental benefits? That comes with its own set of hassles, costs, and risks, but it's certainly worth exploring.

Best,

Anne

The second email, from her colleague Caitlin Lovett, the WinWipe brand manager, read "Cartridge system approved!" Like CleanSpritz, WinWipe sales were in decline, and Lovett's brand team was exploring innovative ways to win back consumers. Together, Lovett and the division product development team had created a prototype of a new sprayer system that could eventually promote use of concentrates across all of the MJ Brenner brands. The sprayer, still in test phase, enabled consumers to switch small cartridges of different cleaning product concentrates in and out of a single spray mechanism.

Beaton clicked on the email, and read the message:

Hi Claire,

I'm so happy to report that the cartridge system we spoke of last month has been approved for production! The team tells me we will be ready to ship in 9–12 months, if all goes well. We didn't get into financial details but it looks like we are going to receive tremendous promotional support from Brenner corporate, and of course we'll benefit from the ancillary promotion of all participating brands. The costs of the launch, meanwhile, will be shared across divisions and brands. At this time, there is only one comparable product on the market.

Thanks very much for your support and advice. I hope we will be working on this together in coming months!

Caitlin

Beaton smiled at Caitlin's enthusiasm. In her previous job, Beaton had led a cross-brand product launch, and that's why Lovett had solicited her advice. The launch had been challenging and fulfilling professionally, but Beaton had not forgotten the frequent launch delays or heated exchanges that revealed conflicting interests of key stakeholders. She made a note to reply to Caitlin in the morning, and added a column entitled "Option 3: Cartridge System" to her white board.

Beaton closed her email and returned to her spreadsheet program. She wanted to provide everyone at Monday's meeting with a comprehensive overview of the four options: (1) base case scenario of maintaining the status quo and waiting; (2) re-launch the 3:1 concentrate; (3) add the 4:1

refill concentrate in recyclable pouch; or (4) add 4:1 refill concentrate in the dissolvable packet. For each option, Beaton would outline:

1. Projected SUs (including scenarios based on her projections and those of the finance department)
2. Projected revenues
3. Projected costs
4. Projected contribution
5. Net profit

In addition, Beaton would provide a short write-up to support her own recommendation for the 2013 product line.

Beaton knew that if her proposed strategy fell short of expectations, a successful future at MJ Brenner—including a year-end bonus and hoped-for promotion to vice president in 2013—was unlikely. There were benefits and risks to each strategy, and Beaton had not yet decided on her final recommendation. Was the most financially secure path necessarily best for her team, for MJ Brenner, and for the environment? What if the finance department was right, and consumers would be reluctant to switch to concentrate despite statements to the contrary? Would the CleanSpritz brand do more harm than good and potentially contribute to a public relations debacle? What were the benefits and risks of doing nothing, while waiting for a more biodegradable formula or cross-company cartridge launch?

Exhibit 1 CleanSpritz 2011 U.S. Sales Volume by Store Type

| | Number of Stores | 2011 Unit Volume | % 2011 Volume | 2011 CleanSpritz Sales Volume Breakdown | |
				CleanSpritz Diluted Spray	CleanSpritz Concentrate
Supermarkets	35,200	8,146,356	36.0%	65%	45%
Mass Merchandisers	25,493	3,620,603	16.0%	15%	17%
Warehouse & Discount	747	2,262,877	10.0%	5%	35%
Small Markets	11,565	5,657,192	25.0%	11%	2%
Convenience	70,244	2,941,740	13.0%	4%	1%
Total	143,249	22,628,768	100.0%	100%	100%

Exhibit 2 CleanSpritz Package Sizes and Prices, 2012

Formulation	Container Size (oz)	Diluted oz per container	Containers/ Case	Uses per container	Standard Units (100 uses) per Container	Standard Units (100 uses) per case	Suggested Unit Retail Price	Average Feature (Sale) Price	Retail Price per SU	Average Feature Price per SU	% Total Sales Volume
Diluted Spray	32	32	12	250	2.5	30.0	$ 5.99	$ 3.19	$ 2.40	$ 1.28	80%
3:1 Concentrate	16	64	24	500	5	120.0	$ 11.49	$ 9.45	$ 2.30	$ 1.89	20%

914-537 | CleanSpritz

Exhibit 3 Consumer Usage Study on Household Cleaners

Selected Results from Household Cleaner Consumer Study*	2008	2011
I am concerned about the impact of chemicals in household cleaners*	55%	70%
I am more worried about the environment than I was a year ago	75%	82%
I have tried, or am aware of, green household cleaners	48%	58%
I like to buy "green" whenever possible (MINTEL)	55%	40%
Cleaning products from natural sources are too expensive	48%	50%
Green cleaners are not as effective as other cleaners	27%	21%
I would be willing to try concentrate:	25%	35%
(of %) Because it's more cost effective	68%	59%
(of %) Because it's better for the environment	32%	41%

*Source for some data based on Mintel Report Household Cleaning: The Consumer, May 2011.

Exhibit 4 Consumer Panel Results, August 2012

Consumer Panel Results August 2012 – Packaging Preference	Pouch	Dissolvable Packet
Number of users	300	300
Would buy concentrate at $5.69	55%	45%
Favorable/Unfavorable comments on package handling	80/20	95/5
Percentage of reused containers that were messy as the result of spillage during product transfer	10%	5%
Packaging ratings (scale of 1–10)		
Transferability	7	9
Environmental friendliness	8	8

Exhibit 5 Product Line Cost Breakdown

	Diluted Spray	3:1 Concentrate	4:1 Recyclable Pouch	4:1 Dissolvable Packet
Chemicals/SU	$ 0.15	$ 0.31	$ 0.14	$ 0.14
Packaging materials/SU	$ 0.25	$ 0.10	$ 0.15	$ 0.19
Manufacturing/SU	$ 0.13	$ 0.11	$ 0.13	$ 0.13
Delivery/SU	$ 0.17	$ 0.16	$ 0.10	$ 0.10
Contractor expense/SU	$ -	$ -	$ 0.08	$ 0.10
Total direct costs/SU	$ 0.70	$ 0.68	$ 0.60	$ 0.66
Cost index	100	97	86	94
SU per container	2.5	5.0	2.5	2.5
Total costs/container	$ 1.75	$ 3.40	$ 1.50	$ 1.65

Exhibit 6 Proposed Retail Price and Trade Margin, 2012

	32 oz diluted spray	16 oz concentrate	6.4 oz concentrate pouch	6.4 oz dissolvable packet
Expected retail price	$ 5.99	$ 11.49	$ 5.69	$ 5.69
Expected retail margin	2%	9%	9%	9%
Manufacturer's selling price	$ 5.87	$ 10.46	$ 5.18	$ 5.18
Standard units per container	2.5	5	2.5	2.5
Retail revenues/SU	$ 2.40	$ 2.30	$ 2.28	$ 2.28
Manufacturer's revenues/SU	$ 2.35	$ 2.09	$ 2.07	$ 2.07

Under Armour—Challenging Nike in Sports Apparel

⊨connect

Arthur A. Thompson
The University of Alabama

Founded in 1996 by former University of Maryland football player Kevin Plank, Under Armour was the originator of performance apparel—gear engineered to keep athletes cool, dry, and light throughout the course of a game, practice, or workout. It started with a simple plan to make a T-shirt that provided compression and "wicked" perspiration from the wearer's skin, thereby regulating body temperature and avoiding the discomfort of sweat-absorbed apparel.

Fifteen years later, with 2011 sales of nearly $1.5 billion, Under Armour had a growing brand presence in the roughly $60 billion multisegment retail market for sports apparel and active wear in the United States. Its interlocking "U" and "A" logo had become almost as familiar and well-known as industry-leader Nike's swoosh. The company had boosted its market share from 0.6 percent in 2003 to an estimated 2.8 percent in 2011, which compared quite favorably with Nike's industry-leading market share of 7.0 percent and the 5.4 percent share of second-ranked adidas.[1]

Founder and CEO Kevin Plank believed Under Armour's potential for long-term growth was exceptional for three reasons: (1) the company had built an incredibly powerful and authentic brand in a relatively short time, (2) there were significant opportunities to expand the company's narrow product lineup and brand name appeal into product categories where it currently had little or no market presence, and (3) the company was only in the early stages of establishing its brand and penetrating markets outside North America.

COMPANY BACKGROUND

Kevin Plank honed his competitive instinct growing up with four older brothers and playing football. As a young teenager, he squirmed under the authority of his mother, who was the town mayor of Kensington, Maryland. When he was a high-school sophomore, he was tossed out of Georgetown Prep for poor academic performance and ended up at Fork Union Military Academy, where he learned to accept discipline and resumed playing high-school football. After graduation, Plank became a walk-on special-teams football player for the University of Maryland in the early 1990s, ending his college career as the special-teams' captain in 1995. Throughout his football career, he regularly experienced the discomfort of practicing on hot days and the unpleasantness of peeling off sweat-soaked cotton T-shirts after practice. At the University of Maryland, Plank sometimes changed the cotton T-shirt under his jersey as it became wet and heavy during the course of a game.

During his later college years and in classic entrepreneurial fashion, Plank hit upon the idea of using newly available moisture-wicking, polyester-blend fabrics to create next-generation, tighter-fitting shirts and undergarments that would make it cooler and more comfortable to engage in strenuous activities during high-temperature conditions.[2] While Plank had a job offer from Prudential Life Insurance at the end of his college days in 1995, he couldn't see himself being happy working in a corporate environment. As he told the author of a 2011 *Fortune* article on Under Armour, "I would have killed myself." Despite a lack of business training, Plank opted to try to make a living selling high-tech microfiber shirts. Plank's vision was to sell innovative, technically advanced apparel products engineered with a special fabric construction that provided supreme moisture management. A year of fabric and product testing produced a synthetic compression T-shirt that was suitable for wear beneath an athlete's uniform or equipment, provided a snug fit (like a second skin) and remained drier and lighter than a traditional cotton shirt. Plank formed KP Sports as a subchapter S corporation in Maryland in 1996 and commenced selling the shirt to athletes and sports teams.

The Company's Early Years

Plank's former teammates at high school, military school, and the University of Maryland included some 40 NFL players that he knew well enough to call and offer them the shirt he had come up with. He worked the phone and, with a trunk full of shirts in the back of his car, visited schools and training camps in person to show his products. Within a short time, Plank's sales successes were good enough that he convinced Kip Fulks, who played lacrosse at Maryland, to become a partner in his enterprise. Fulks' initial role was to leverage his connections to promote use of the company's shirts by lacrosse players. Their sales strategy was predicated on networking and referrals. But Fulks had another critical role—he had good credit and was able to obtain 17 credit cards that were used to make purchases from suppliers and charge expenses.[3] Operations were conducted on a shoestring budget out of the basement of Plank's grandmother's house in Georgetown, a Washington, D.C. suburb. Plank and Fulks generated sufficient cash from their sales efforts and Fulks never missed a minimum payment on any of his credit cards. When cash flows became particularly tight, Plank's older brother Scott made loans to the company to help keep KP Sports afloat (in 2011, Scott owned 4 percent of the company's stock). It didn't take long for Plank and Fulks to learn that it was more productive to direct their sales efforts more toward equipment managers than to individual players. Getting a whole team to adopt use of the T-shirts that KP Sports was marketing meant convincing equipment managers that it was more economical to provide players with a pricey $25 high-performance T-shirt that would hold up better in the long-run than a cheap cotton T-shirt.

In 1998, the company's sales revenues and growth prospects were sufficient to secure a $250,000 small-business loan from a tiny bank in Washington, D.C.; the loan enabled the company to move its basement operation to a facility on Sharp Street in nearby Baltimore.[4] As sales continued to gain momentum, the D.C. bank later granted KP Sports additional small loans from time to time to help fund its needs for more working capital. Then Ryan Wood, one of Plank's acquaintances from high school, joined the company in 1999 and became a partner. The company consisted of three jocks trying to gain a foothold in a growing, highly competitive industry against some 25 + brands, including those of Nike, adidas, Columbia, and Patagonia. Plank functioned as president and CEO, Kip Fulks was vice president of sourcing and quality assurance, and Ryan Wood was vice president of sales.

Nonetheless, KP Sports' sales grew briskly as it expanded its product line to include high-tech undergarments tailored for athletes in different sports and for cold temperatures as well as hot temperatures, plus jerseys, team uniforms, socks, and other accessories. Increasingly, the company was able to secure deals not just to provide gear for a particular team but for most or all of a school's sports teams. However, the company's partners came to recognize the merits of tapping the retail market for high-performance apparel and began making sales calls on sports apparel retailers. In 2000, Galyan's, a large retail chain since acquired by Dick's Sporting Goods, signed on to carry KP Sports's expanding line of performance apparel for men, women, and youths. Sales to other sports apparel retailers began to explode, quickly making the retail segment of the sports apparel market the biggest component of the company's revenue stream. Revenues totaled $5.3 million in 2000, with an operating income of $0.7 million. The company's products were available in some 500 retail stores. Beginning in 2000, Scott Plank joined the company as vice president of finance, with operational and strategic responsibilities as well.

Rapid Growth Ensues

Over the next 11 years, the company's product line evolved to include a widening variety of shirts, shorts, underwear, outerwear, gloves, and other offerings. The strategic intent was to grow the business by replacing products made with cotton and other traditional fabrics with innovatively designed performance products that incorporated a variety of technologically advanced fabrics and specialized manufacturing techniques, all in an attempt to make the wearer feel "drier, lighter, and more comfortable." In 1999, the company began selling its products in Japan through a licensee. On January 1, 2002, prompted by growing operational complexities, increased financial requirements, and plans for further geographic expansion, KP Sports revoked its "S" corporation status and became a "C" corporation. The company opened a Canadian sales office in 2003 and began efforts to grow its market presence in Canada. In 2004, KP Sports became the outfitter of the University of Maryland football team and was a supplier to some 400 women's sports teams at NCAA Division 1-A colleges and universities. The company used independent sales agents to begin selling its products in the United Kingdom in 2005. SportsScanINFO estimated that as of 2004, KP Sports had a 73 percent share of the U.S. market for compression tops and bottoms, more than seven times that of its nearest competitor.[5]

Broadening demand for the company's product offerings among professional, collegiate, and Olympic teams and athletes, active outdoor enthusiasts, elite tactical professionals and consumers with active lifestyles propelled revenue growth from $5.3 million in 2000 to $263.4 million for the 12 months ending September 30, 2005, equal to a compound annual growth rate of 127 percent. Operating income increased from $0.7 million in 2000 to $32.7 million during the same period, a compound annual growth rate of 124 percent. About 90 percent of the company revenues came from sales to some 6,000 retail stores in the United States and 2,000 stores in Canada, Japan, and the United Kingdom. In addition, sales were being made to high-profile athletes and teams, most notably in the National Football League, Major League Baseball, the National Hockey League, and major collegiate and Olympic sports. KP Sports had 574 employees at the end of September 2005.

Throughout 2005, KP Sports increased its offerings to include additional men's and women's performance products and, in particular, began entry into such off-field outdoor sports segments as hunting, fishing, running, mountain sports, skiing, and golf. Management expected that its new product offerings in 2006 would include football cleats.

KP Sports Is Renamed Under Armour

In late 2005, the company changed its name to Under Armour and became a public company with an initial public offering of 9.5 million shares of Class A common stock that generated net proceeds of approximately $114.9 million. Simultaneously, existing stockholders sold 2.6 million shares of Class A stock from their personal holdings. The shares were all sold at just above the offer price of $13 per share. On the first day of trading after the IPO, the shares closed at $25.30, after opening at $31 per share. Following these initial sales of Under Armour stock to the general public, Under Armour's outstanding shares of common stock consisted of two classes: Class A common stock and Class B common stock; both classes were identical in all respects except for voting and conversion rights. Holders of Class A common stock were entitled to one vote per share, and holders of Class B common stock were entitled to 10 votes per share, on all matters to be voted on by common stockholders. Shares of Class A and Class B common stock voted together as a single class on all matters submitted to a vote of stockholders. All of the Class B common stock was beneficially owned by Kevin Plank, which represented 83.0 percent of the combined voting power of all of the outstanding common stock. As a result, Plank was able to control the outcome of substantially all matters submitted to a stockholder vote, including the election of directors, amendments to Under Armour's charter, and mergers or other business combinations.

At the time of Under Armour's IPO, Kevin Plank, Kip Fulks, and Ryan Wood were all 33 years old; Scott Plank was 39 years old. After the IPO, Kevin Plank owned 15.2 million shares of Under Armour's Class A shares (and all of the Class B shares); Kip Fulks owned 2.125 million Class A shares, Ryan Wood owned 2.142 million Class A shares, and Scott Plank owned 3.95 million Class A shares. All four had opted to sell a small fraction of their common shares at the time of the IPO—these accounted for a combined 1.83 million of the 2.6 million shares sold from the holdings of various directors, officers, and other entities. Ryan Wood decided to leave his position as senior vice president of sales at Under Armour in 2007 to run a cattle farm. Kip Fulks assumed the position of chief operating officer at Under Armour in September 2011, after moving up the executive ranks in several capacities, chiefly those related to sourcing, quality assurance, product development, and product innovation. In 2011, Scott Plank was the company's executive vice president of business development and focused on domestic and international business development opportunities. Prior to that, he served as senior vice president of retail from March 2006 to July 2009 with responsibility for retail outlet and specialty stores and e-commerce, as chief administrative officer from January 2004 to February 2006, and vice president of finance from 2000 to 2003.

EXHIBIT 1   Selected Financial Data for Under Armour, Inc., 2006–2011 (in 000s, except per-share amounts)

	Years Ending December 31				
Selected Income Statement Data	2011	2010	2009	2008	2006
Net revenues	$1,472,684	$1,063,927	$856,411	$725,244	$430,689
Cost of goods sold	759,848	533,420	446,286	372,203	216,753
Gross profit	712,836	530,507	410,125	353,041	213,936
Selling, general and administrative expenses	550,069	418,152	324,852	276,116	157,018
Income from operations	162,767	112,355	85,273	76,925	56,918
Interest expense, net	(3,841)	(2,258)	(2,344)	(850)	1,457
Other expense, net	(2,064)	(1,178)	(511)	(6,175)	712
Income before income taxes	156,862	108,919	82,418	69,900	59,087
Provision for income taxes	59,943	40,442	35,633	31,671	20,108
Net income	$ 96,919	$ 68,477	$ 46,785	$ 38,229	$ 38,979
Net income per common share					
Basic	$1.88	$1.35	$0.94	$0.78	$0.82
Diluted	1.85	1.34	0.92	0.76	0.78
Weighted average common shares outstanding					
Basic	51,570	50,798	49,848	49,086	47,291
Diluted	52,526	51,282	50,650	50,342	49,676
Selected Balance Sheet Data (in 000s)					
Cash and cash equivalents	$175,384	$203,870	$187,297	$102,042	$70,655
Working capital*	506,056	406,703	327,838	263,313	173,389
Inventories at year-end	324,409	215,355	148,488	182,232	81,031
Total assets	919,210	675,378	545,588	487,555	289,368
Total debt and capital lease obligations, including current maturities	77,724	15,942	20,223	45,591	6,257
Total stockholders' equity	636,432	496,966	399,997	331,097	214,388
Selected Cash Flow Data					
Net cash provided by operating activities	$15,218	$50,114	$119,041	$69,516	$10,701

* Working capital is defined as current assets minus current liabilities.

Source: Company 10-K reports 2011, 2010, and 2008.

Exhibit 1 summarizes Under Armour's financial performance in the six years following the company's 2005 IPO. The company stock was trading in the $72 to $78 range in January 2012. Following the announcement of better-than-expected first quarter 2012 earnings and management forecasts of full-year 2012 revenues of $1.78 to $1.80 billion, Under Armour's stock climbed to $102.70 per share in the last week of April 2012.

UNDER ARMOUR'S STRATEGY

Under Armour's mission was "to make all athletes better through passion, design, and the relentless pursuit of innovation." The company's principal business activities in 2012 were the development, marketing, and distribution of branded performance apparel, footwear, and accessories for men, women, and youths. The brand's moisture-wicking fabrications were engineered

EXHIBIT 2   **Composition of Under Armour's Revenues, 2009–2011**

A. **Net revenues by product category** (in thousands of $)

	2011		2010		2009	
	Dollars	Percent	Dollars	Percent	Dollars	Percent
Apparel	$1,122,031	76.2%	$ 853,493	80.2%	$651,779	76.1%
Footwear	181,684	12.3	127,175	12.0	136,224	15.9
Accessories	132,400	9.0	43,882	4.1	35,077	4.1
Total net sales	1,436,115	97.5%	$1,024,550	96.3%	$823,080	96.1%
License revenues	36,569	2.5	39,377	3.7	33,331	3.9
Total net revenues	$1,472,684	100.0%	$1,063,927	100.0%	$856,411	100.0%

B. **Net revenues by geographic region** (in thousands of $)

	2011		2010		2009	
	Dollars	Percent	Dollars	Percent	Dollars	Percent
North America	$1,383,346	93.9%	$ 997,816	93.7%	$808,020	94.3%
Other foreign countries	89,338	6.1	66,111	6.3	48,391	5.7
Total net revenues	$1,472,684	100.0%	$1,063,927	100.0%	$856,411	100.0%

Source: Company 10-K reports, 2011 and 2010.

in many designs and styles for wear in nearly every climate to provide a performance alternative to traditional products. Its products were worn by athletes at all levels, from youth to professional, and by consumers with active lifestyles. Over 90 percent of Under Armour's sales were in North America, but international sales to distributors and retailers outside North America were growing. Exhibit 2 shows the composition of Under Armour's revenues.

Growth Strategy

Under Armour's growth strategy in early 2012 consisted of several strategic initiatives:

- Continuing to broaden the company's product offerings to men, women, and youths for wear in a widening variety of sports and recreational activities.
- Targeting additional consumer segments for the company's ever-expanding lineup of performance products.
- Securing additional distribution of Under Armour products in the retail marketplace in North America via not only store retailers and catalog retailers but also through Under Armour factory outlet and specialty stores and sales at the company's website.

- Expanding the sale of Under Armour products in foreign countries and becoming a global competitor in the world market for sports apparel and performance products.
- Growing global awareness of the Under Armour brand name and strengthening the appeal of Under Armour products worldwide.

Product Line Strategy

Under Armour's diverse product offerings in 2012 consisted of apparel, footwear, and accessories for men, women, and youths marketed at multiple price levels in a variety of styles and fits intended to regulate body temperature and enhance comfort, mobility, and performance regardless of weather conditions.

Apparel The company designed and merchandised three lines of apparel gear: HeatGear® for hot weather conditions; ColdGear® for cold weather conditions; and AllSeasonGear® for temperature conditions between the extremes.

HeatGear HeatGear was designed to be worn in warm to hot temperatures under equipment or as a single layer. The company's first compression T-shirt was the original HeatGear product and remained its signature style in 2012. In sharp contrast to a sweat-soaked cotton T-shirt that could weigh two to three pounds, HeatGear was engineered with a microfiber blend featuring what Under Armour termed a "Moisture Transport System" that ensured the body will stay cool, dry, and light. HeatGear was offered in a variety of tops and bottoms in a broad array of colors and styles for wear in the gym or outside in warm weather. Compression-fit HeatGear reduced muscle fatigue, was particularly popular for training sessions and competition, and was the company's top-selling gear line year-round.

ColdGear Under Armour high-performance fabrics were appealing to people participating in cold-weather sports and vigorous recreational activities like snow skiing who needed both warmth and moisture-wicking protection from a sometimes overheated body. ColdGear was designed to wick moisture from the body while circulating body heat from hotspots to maintain a core body temperature. All ColdGear apparel provided dry warmth in a single light layer that could be worn beneath a jersey, uniform, protective gear or ski-vest, or other cold weather outerwear. ColdGear products generally were sold at higher price levels than other Under Armour gear lines.

AllSeasonGear AllSeasonGear was designed to be worn in changing temperatures and used technical fabrics to keep the wearer cool and dry in warmer temperatures while preventing a chill in cooler temperatures.

Each of the three apparel lines contained three fit types: compression (tight fit), fitted (athletic fit) and loose (relaxed).

Footwear   Under Armour began marketing footwear products for men, women, and youths in 2006 and had expanded its footwear line every year since. Currently, its offerings included football, baseball, lacrosse, softball and soccer cleats, slides, performance training footwear, running footwear, basketball footwear, and hunting boots. Under Armour's athletic footwear was innovatively designed to provide stabilization, directional cushioning, and moisture management, and was engineered to be light and breathable and to maximize the athlete's comfort and control.

Accessories   Under Armour's accessory line in 2012 included gloves, socks, headwear, bags, knee-pads, custom-molded mouth guards, and eyewear designed to be used and worn before, during, and after competition.

All of these featured performance advantages and functionality similar to other Under Armour products. For instance, the company's baseball batting, football, golf, and running gloves included HeatGear and ColdGear technologies and were designed with advanced fabrications to provide various high-performance attributes that differentiated its gloves from those of rival brands.

Under Armour had entered into licensing agreements with a number of firms to produce and market some of its accessories (bags, headgear, and socks). In these instances, Under Armour product, marketing, and sales teams were actively involved in all steps of the design process in order to maintain brand standards and consistency. By 2011, however, Under Armour had developed its own headwear and bag accessories and began selling them itself rather than through licensees. Revenues generated from the sale of all licensed accessories are included in the licensing revenue amounts shown in Exhibit 2A.

Marketing, Promotion, and Brand Management Strategies

Under Armour had an in-house marketing and promotions department that designed and produced most of its advertising campaigns to drive consumer demand for its products and build awareness of Under Armour as a leading performance athletic brand. The company's total marketing expenses, including endorsements and advertising, were $167.9 million in 2011, $128.2 million in 2010, and $108.9 million in 2009. These totals included the costs of sponsoring events and various sports teams, the costs of athlete endorsements, and advertising expenses.

Sports Marketing   A key element of Under Armour's marketing and promotion strategy was to promote the sales and use of its products to high-performing athletes and teams on the high school, collegiate, and professional levels. This strategy included entering into outfitting agreements with a variety of collegiate and professional sports teams, sponsoring an assortment of collegiate and professional sports events, and selling Under Armour products directly to team equipment managers and to individual athletes.

Management believed that having audiences see Under Armour products (with the interlocking UA logo prominently displayed) being worn by athletes on the playing field helped the company establish on-field authenticity of the Under Armour brand with consumers. Considerable effort went into giving

C-48   Part 2   Cases in Crafting and Executing Strategy

EXHIBIT 3   The Under Armour Logo and Its Use on Selected Under Armour Products

Under Armour products broad exposure at live sporting events, as well as on television, in magazines, and on a wide variety of Internet sites. Exhibit 3 shows a sampling of the Under Armour logo and its use on Under Armour products.

In 2011, Under Armour was the official outfitter of *all* the athletic teams at Boston College, Texas Tech University, the University of Maryland, the University of South Carolina, Auburn University, and the University of South Florida and *selected* sports teams at the University of Illinois, Northwestern University, the University of Delaware, the University of Hawaii,

Southern Illinois University, Wagner College, Whittier College, and La Salle University. All told, it was the official outfitter of over 100 Division I men's and women's collegiate athletic teams, rapidly growing numbers (over 40) of high school athletic teams, and several Olympic sports teams; and it supplied sideline apparel and fan gear for many collegiate teams as well. In addition, Under Armour sold products to high profile professional athletes and teams, most notably in the National Football League, Major League Baseball, and the National Hockey League. Since 2006, Under Armour had been an official supplier of football cleats to the National Football League (NFL). In 2010, it signed an agreement to become an official supplier of gloves to the NFL beginning in 2011 and to supply the NFL with training apparel for athletes attending NFL tryout camps beginning in 2012.

Internationally, Under Armour was building its brand image by selling products to European soccer and rugby teams. It was the official supplier of performance apparel to the Hannover 96 football club and the Welsh Rugby Union, among others. In addition, it was an official supplier of performance apparel to Hockey Canada, had advertising rights at many locations in the Air Canada Center during the Toronto Maple Leafs' home games, and was the Official Performance Product Sponsor of the Toronto Maple Leafs.

Under Armour also had sponsorship agreements with individual athletes. Its strategy was to secure the endorsement of such newly emerging sports stars as Milwaukee Bucks point guard Brandon Jennings, U.S. professional skier and Olympic gold medal winner Lindsey Vonn, professional lacrosse player Paul Rabil, Baltimore Orioles catcher Matthew Wieters, 2010 National League Rookie of the Year Buster Posey, UFC Welterweight Champion Georges St-Pierre, the number one pick in the 2010 Major League Baseball Draft (Bryce Harper of the Washington Nationals), NBA rookie Kemba Walker, and the number 2 pick in the 2001 NBA draft (Derrick Williams). In addition, the company's roster of athletes included established stars: NFL football players Tom Brady, Ray Lewis, Brandon Jacobs, Miles Austin, Vernon Davis, and Anquan Boldin; triathlon champion Chris "Macca" McCormack; professional baseball players Ryan Zimmerman and Jose Reyes; U.S. Women's National Soccer Team players Heather Mitts and Lauren Cheney; U.S. Olympic and professional volleyball player Nicole Branagh; U.S. Olympic swimmer Michael Phelps; and professional golfer Hunter Mahan.

In 2010, Under Armour hosted over 50 combines, camps, and clinics for male and female athletes in many sports at various regional sites in the United States. It sponsored American Youth Football (an organization that promoted the development of youth), the Under Armour All-America Football Game (a nationally televised annual competition between the top seniors in high school football), the Under Armour Senior Bowl (a televised annual competition between the top seniors in college football), The Under Armour (Baltimore) Marathon, The Under Armour All-America Lacrosse Classic, and the All-America games in softball and volleyball for elite high school athletes. Under

Armour had partnered with Ripken Baseball to outfit some 35,000 Ripken Baseball participants and to be the title sponsor for all 25 Ripken youth baseball tournaments. It had partnered with the Baseball Factory to outfit top high school baseball athletes from head to toe and serve as the title sponsor for nationally recognized baseball tournaments and teams. In addition, it was the presenting sponsor for the 2010 NFL Scouting Combine and, beginning with the 2011 season, Under Armour became the Official Footwear Supplier of Major League Baseball.

Under Armour spent approximately $43.5 million in 2011 for athlete endorsements and various sponsorships, compared to about $29.4 million in 2010. The company was contractually obligated to spend a *minimum* of $52.9 million for endorsements and sponsorships during 2012, and at least an additional $115.7 million during 2013–2017.[6] The company did not know precisely what its future sponsorship costs for individual athletes would be because its contractual agreements with these athletes were subject to certain performance-based variables.

Retail Marketing and Product Presentation   The primary thrust of Under Armour's retail marketing strategy was to increase the floor space *exclusively* dedicated to Under Armour products in the stores of its major retail accounts. The key initiative here was to design and fund Under Armour "concept shops"—including flooring, in-store fixtures, product displays, life-size athlete mannequins, and lighting—within the stores of its major retail customers. This shop-in-shop approach was seen as an effective way to gain the placement of Under Armour products in prime floor space, educate consumers about Under Armour products, and create a more engaging and sales-producing way for consumers to shop for Under Armour products.

In stores that did not have Under Armour concept shops, Under Armour worked with retailers to establish optimal placement of its products. In "big-box" sporting goods stores, it was important to be sure that the growing variety of Under Armour products was represented in all of the various departments (hunting apparel in the hunting goods department, footwear and socks in the footwear department, and so on). Except for the retail stores with Under Armour concept shops, company personnel worked with retailers to employ in-store fixtures and displays that highlighted the UA logo and conveyed a performance-oriented, athletic look (chiefly through the use of life-size athlete mannequins). The idea was not only to enhance the visibility of Under Armour products but also reinforce the message that the company's brand was distinct from those of competitors.

Media and Promotion Under Armour advertised in a variety of national digital, broadcast, and print media outlets and its advertising campaigns included a variety of lengths and formats. The company's "Protect this House" and "Click-Clack" campaigns featured several NFL players, and its "Protect this House" campaign had been used in several NFL and collegiate stadiums during games as a crowd prompt. A related ad campaign, "Protect this House.* I Will," focused heavily on the training aspect of sports. On several occasions, the company had secured the use of Under Armour products in movies, television shows, and video games; management believed the appearance of Under Armour products in these media reinforced authenticity of the brand and provided brand exposure to audiences that may not have seen Under Armour's other advertising campaigns. In 2011, Under Armour significantly grew the company's "fan base" via social sites like Facebook and Twitter, surpassing the million-fan mark and bringing attention to what management considered as the company's most compelling brand stories.

Distribution Strategy

Under Armour products were available in over 25,000 retail stores worldwide at the end of 2011, of which about 18,000 retail stores were in North America. Under Armour also sold its products directly to consumers through its own factory outlet and specialty stores, website, and catalogs.

Wholesale Distribution In 2011, 70 percent of Under Armour's net revenues were generated from sales to retailers. The company's principal customers included Dick's Sporting Goods, about 18 percent of sales), The Sports Authority (about 8 percent of sales), Academy Sports and Outdoors, Hibbett Sporting Goods, Modell's Sporting Goods, Bass Pro Shops, Cabela's, Footlocker, Finish Line, and The Army and Air Force Exchange Service. In Canada, the company's biggest customers were Sportchek International and Sportman International. Roughly 75 percent of all sales made to retailers were to large-format national and regional retail chains. The remaining 25 percent of wholesale sales were to lesser-sized outdoor and other specialty retailers, institutional athletic departments, leagues, teams, and fitness specialists. Independent

and specialty retailers were serviced by a combination of in-house sales personnel and third-party commissioned manufacturer's representatives.

Direct-to-Consumer Sales In late 2007, Under Armour opened its first company-owned retail location at the Westfield Annapolis mall in Annapolis, Maryland. In May 2008, Under Armour also opened a larger 6,000-square-foot store at Westfield Fox Valley in Aurora, Illinois (a Chicago suburb). Going into 2012, the company had five Under Armour specialty stores (in Annapolis; Aurora; Natick, Massachusetts—a Boston suburb; Bethesda, Maryland; and Vail, Colorado) and 80 factory outlet locations in 34 states. The first Under Armour specialty store outside of North America was opened in Edinburgh, Scotland—it was owned and operated by First XV, a rugby store that was situated next door. In 2012, Under Armour opened a 25,000-square-foot showroom and retail store at its Tide Point headquarters in Baltimore, Maryland. In 2011, 27 percent of Under Armour's net revenues were generated through direct-to-consumer sales, including discounted sales at its factory outlet stores and sales through its specialty stores, global website (www. ua.com), and catalog.

Product Licensing About 3 percent of the company's net revenues came from licensing arrangements to manufacture and distribute Under Armour branded products. Under Armour pre-approved all products manufactured and sold by its licensees, and the company's quality assurance team strived to ensure that licensed products met the same quality and compliance standards as company-sold products. In 2012, Under Armour had relationships with several licensees for team uniforms, eyewear, and custom-molded mouth guards, as well as the distribution of Under Armour products to college bookstores and golf pro shops. In addition, Under Armour had a relationship with a Japanese licensee, Dome Corporation, that had the exclusive rights to distribute Under Armour products in Japan. Dome sold Under Armour products to professional baseball and soccer teams (including Omiya Ardija, a professional soccer club in Saitama, Japan) and to over 2,000 independent specialty stores and large sporting goods retailers, such as Alpen, Himaraya, The Sports Authority, and Xebio. Under Armour made a minority equity investment in Dome Corporation in January 2011.

Distribution Outside North America Because Under Armour management was convinced that the trend toward using performance products was global, it had begun entering foreign country markets as rapidly as was prudent. A European headquarters was opened in 2006 in Amsterdam, The Netherlands, to conduct and oversee sales, marketing, and logistics activities across Europe. The strategy was to first sell Under Armour products directly to teams and athletes and then leverage visibility in the sports segment to access broader audiences of potential consumers. By 2011, Under Armour had succeeded in selling products to Premier League Football clubs and multiple running, golf, and cricket clubs in the United Kingdom, soccer teams in France, Germany, Greece, Ireland, Italy, Spain, and Sweden, as well as First Division Rugby clubs in France, Ireland, Italy, and the United Kingdom.

Sales to European retailers quickly followed on the heels of gains being made in the sports team segment. In 2012, Under Armour had 4,000 retail customers in Austria, France, Germany, Ireland, and the United Kingdom and was generating revenues from third-party distributors who sold Under Armour products to retailers in Australia, Italy, Greece, Scandinavia, and Spain. In 2010–2011, sales efforts commenced in Latin America and Asia. In Latin America, Under Armour sold directly to retailers in some countries and in other countries sold its products to independent distributors who then were responsible for securing sales to retailers. In 2011, Under Armour opened a specialty store in Shanghai, China, to begin learning about Chinese consumers.

Product Design and Development

UA products were manufactured with technical fabrications produced by third parties and developed in collaboration with the company's product development team. Under Armour favored the use of superior, technically advanced fabrics, produced to its specifications, and focused its product development efforts on design, fit, climate, and product end-use. The company regularly upgraded its products as next-generation fabrics when better performance characteristics became available and as the needs of athletes changed. Product development efforts also aimed at broadening the company's product offerings in both new and existing product categories and market segments. An effort was made to design products with "visible technology," utilizing color, texture, and fabrication that would enhance customers' perception and understanding of the use and benefits of Under Armour products.

Under Armour's product development team had significant prior industry experience at leading fabric and other raw material suppliers and branded athletic apparel and footwear companies throughout the world. The team worked closely with Under Armour's sports marketing and sales teams as well as professional and collegiate athletes to identify product trends and determine market needs. Collaboration among the company's product development, sales, and sports marketing team had proved important in identifying the opportunity and market for the recently introduced Catalyst products (made from 100 percent recycled plastic bottles) that were the cornerstone of the Under Armour Green Collection.

Sourcing, Manufacturing, and Quality Assurance

Many of the technically advanced specialty fabrics and other raw materials used in UA products were developed by third parties and, typically, were available only from a limited number of sources. In 2011, approximately 50 to 55 percent of the fabric used in UA products came from six suppliers, with locations in Malaysia, Mexico, Peru, Taiwan, and the United States. Because a big fraction of the materials used in UA products were petroleum-based synthetics, the costs of the fabrics sourced from suppliers were subject to crude oil price fluctuations. Beginning in 2011, Under Armour introduced a line of Charged Cotton™ products that incorporated cotton fabrics subject to price fluctuations and varying cotton harvests.

In 2011, substantially all UA products were manufactured by 23 primary manufacturers, operating in 16 countries; seven manufacturers produced approximately 45 percent of UA's products. Approximately 60 percent were manufactured in Asia, 22 percent in Central and South America, 8 percent in Mexico, and 8 percent in the Middle East. All manufacturers used only fabrics preapproved by Under Armour, and all were evaluated for quality systems, social compliance, and financial strength by Under Armour's quality assurance team, prior to being selected and also on an ongoing basis. Under Armour required its contract manufacturers to adhere to a code of conduct regarding quality of manufacturing, working conditions, and other social concerns. The company strived to qualify multiple manufacturers for particular product types and fabrications and to seek out vendors that could perform multiple manufacturing stages, such as procuring raw materials and providing finished products, which helped UA control its cost of goods sold. The company had an office in Hong Kong to support its manufacturing, quality assurance, and sourcing efforts for apparel, and offices in Guangzhou, China, to support its manufacturing, quality assurance, and sourcing efforts for footwear.

Under Armour had a 17,000-square-foot Special Make-Up Shop located at one of its distribution facilities in Maryland where it had the capability to make and ship customized apparel products on tight deadlines for high-profile athletes, leagues, and teams. While these apparel products represented a tiny fraction of Under Armour's revenues, management believed the facility helped provide superior service to an important customer segment.

Distribution Facilities and Inventory Management

Under Armour packaged and shipped the majority of its products for the North American market at two distribution facilities located approximately 15 miles from its Baltimore, Maryland, headquarters. One was a 359,000-square-foot facility built in 2000 and the other was a 308,000-square-foot facility; both were leased. In addition, the company utilized the services of a third-party logistics provider with primary locations in California and in Florida; the company's agreement with this provider was set to expire in December 2013. Distribution to European customers was handled by a third-party logistics provider based in Venlo, The Netherlands. Under Armour had contracted with a third-party logistics provider to handle packing and shipment to customers in Asia. Management expected that the company would add additional distribution facilities in the future.

Under Armour based the amount of inventory it needed to have on hand for each item in its product line on existing orders, anticipated sales, and the need to rapidly deliver orders to customers. Its inventory strategy was focused on (1) having sufficient inventory to fill incoming orders promptly and (2) putting strong systems and procedures in place to improve the efficiency with which it managed its inventories of individual products and total inventory. The amounts of seasonal products it ordered from manufacturers were based on current bookings, the need to ship seasonal items at the start of the shipping window in order to maximize the floor space productivity of retail customers, and the need to adequately stock its factory outlet stores. Excess inventories of particular products were either shipped to its factory outlet stores or earmarked for sale to third-party liquidators.

However, the growing number of individual items in UA's product line and uncertainties surrounding upcoming consumer demand for individual items made it difficult to accurately forecast how many units to order from manufacturers and what the appropriate stocking requirements were for many items. Under Armour's year-end inventories rose from $148.4 million in 2009 to $215.4 million in 2010 to $324.4 million in 2011—percentage increases that exceeded the gains in companywide revenues and that caused days of inventories to climb from 121.4 days in 2009 to 148.4 days in 2010 and to 155.8 days in 2011. The increases were due, in part, to long lead-times for design and production of some products and from having to begin manufacturing many products before receiving any orders for them. In January 2012, management announced that because inventory growth of 118 percent over the past two years had outstripped revenue growth of 72 percent, it was instituting a review of UA's entire product line and was contemplating cutbacks in the number of products offered, perhaps by as much as 20 percent.

COMPETITION

The multisegment global market for sports apparel, athletic footwear, and related accessories was fragmented among some 25 brand-name competitors with diverse product lines and varying geographic coverage and numerous small competitors with specialized-use apparel lines that usually operated within a single country or geographic region. Industry participants included athletic and leisure shoe companies, athletic and leisure apparel companies, sports equipment companies, and large companies having diversified lines of athletic and leisure shoes, apparel, and equipment. In 2011, the global market for athletic footwear was about $65 billion, and the global market for sports apparel was approximately $125 billion. Nike was the clear market leader, with a footwear market share of about 17 percent and a sports apparel share of about 4.4 percent. Other prominent competitors besides Under Armour included adidas, Puma, Columbia, Fila, and Polo Ralph Lauren. Exhibit 4 shows a representative sample of the best-known companies and brands.

Competition was intense and revolved around performance and reliability, new product development, price, product identity through marketing and promotion, and customer support and service. It was common for the leading companies to actively sponsor sporting events and clinics and to contract with prominent and influential athletes, coaches, teams,

EXHIBIT 4   Major Competitors and Brands in Selected Segments of the Sports Apparel, Athletic Footwear, and Accessory Industry, 2012

Performance Apparel for Sports (baseball, football, basketball, softball, volleyball, hockey, lacrosse, soccer, track & field, and other action sports)	Performance-Driven Athletic Footwear	Training/Fitness Clothing
• Nike • Under Armour • Eastbay • adidas • Russell	• Nike • Reebok • adidas • New Balance • Saucony • Puma • Rockport • Converse • Ryka • Asics	• Nike • Under Armour • Eastbay • adidas • Puma • Fila • Lululemon athletica • Champion • Asics • SUGOI

Performance Activewear and Sports-Inspired Lifestyle Apparel	Performance Skiwear	Performance Golf Apparel
• Polo Ralph Lauren • Lacoste • Izod • Cutter & Buck • Timberland	• Salomon • North Face • Descente • Columbia • Patagonia • Marmot • Helly Hansen • Bogner • Spyder • Many others	• Footjoy • Polo Golf • Nike • adidas • Puma • Under Armour • Ashworth • Cutter & Buck • Greg Norman • Many others

colleges, and sports leagues to endorse their brands and use their products.

Nike, Inc.

Incorporated in 1968, Nike was engaged in the design, development, and worldwide marketing and selling of footwear, sports apparel, sports equipment, and accessory products. Its principal businesses in 2012 are shown in the table at the bottom of this page.

Total companywide sales were $20.9 billion in fiscal 2011. Nike was the world's largest seller of athletic footwear and athletic apparel, with over 40,000

Businesses	Fiscal 2011 Sales
Nike Brand footwear (over 800 models and styles)	$11,493 million
Nike Brand apparel	5,475
Nike Brand equipment for a wide variety of sports	1,013
Converse (a designer and marketer of athletic footwear, apparel, and accessories)	1,130
Nike Golf (footwear, apparel, golf equipment, accessories)	623
Cole Haan (a designer and marketer of dress and casual footwear, apparel, and accessories for men and women)	518
Hurley (a designer and marketer of action sports and youth lifestyle footwear and apparel, including shorts, tees, tanks, hoodies, and swimwear)	252
Umbro (a prominent British-based global provider of soccer apparel and equipment)	224

EXHIBIT 5   Nike's Worldwide Retail and Distribution Network, 2011

United States	Foreign Countries
• ~20,000 retail accounts	• More than 20,000 retail accounts
• 150 Nike factory outlet stores	• 243 Nike factory outlet stores
• 16 Nike stores	• 50 Nike stores
• 9 NIKETOWN stores	• 3 NIKETOWN stores
• 3 distribution centers	• 16 distribution centers
• Company website (www.nikestore.com)	• Independent distributors and licensees in over 170 countries
	• Company website (www.nikestore.com)

retail accounts, over 470 company-owned stores, 19 distribution centers, and selling arrangements with independent distributors and licensees in over 170 countries (see Exhibit 5). About 57 percent of Nike's sales came from outside the United States. Nike's retail account base in the U.S. included a mix of footwear stores, sporting goods stores, athletic specialty stores, department stores, skate, tennis and golf shops, and other retail accounts. During fiscal 2011, Nike's three largest customers accounted for approximately 23 percent of U.S. sales in the United States; its three largest customers outside the U.S. accounted for 9 percent of total non-U.S. sales. In fiscal 2011, Nike had sales of $3.2 billion at its company-owned stores and website.

Principal Products   Nike's athletic footwear models and styles were designed primarily for specific athletic use, although many were worn for casual or leisure purposes. Running, training, basketball, soccer, sport-inspired casual shoes, and kids' shoes were the company's top-selling footwear categories. It also marketed footwear designed for baseball, cheerleading, football, golf, lacrosse, outdoor activities, skateboarding, tennis, volleyball, walking, and wrestling. The company designed and marketed Nike-branded sports apparel and accessories for most all of these same sports categories, as well as sports-inspired lifestyle apparel, athletic bags, and accessory items. Footwear, apparel, and accessories were often marketed in "collections" of similar design or for specific purposes. It also marketed apparel with licensed college and professional team and league logos. Nike-brand offerings in sporting equipment included bags, socks, sport balls, eyewear, timepieces, electronic devices, bats, gloves, protective equipment, and golf clubs.

Exhibit 6 shows a breakdown of Nike's sales of footwear, apparel, and equipment by geographic region for fiscal years 2009–2011.

Marketing, Promotions, and Endorsements   Nike responded to trends and shifts in consumer preferences by (1) adjusting the mix of existing product offerings, (2) developing new products, styles, and categories, and (3) striving to influence sports and fitness preferences through aggressive marketing, promotional activities, sponsorships, and athlete endorsements. Nike spent $2.45 billion in fiscal 2011, $2.36 billion in fiscal 2010, and $2.35 billion for what it termed "demand creation expenses" that included advertising and promotion expenses and the costs of endorsement contracts. Well over 500 professional, collegiate, club, and Olympic sports teams in football, basketball, baseball, ice hockey, soccer, rugby, speed skating, tennis, swimming, and other sports wore Nike uniforms with the Nike swoosh prominently visible. There were over 1,000 prominent professional athletes with Nike endorsement contracts in 2011–2012, including NFL players Drew Brees, Tim Tebow, Tony Romo, Aaron Rodgers, and Clay Mathews; Major League Baseball players Albert Pujols and Alex Rodriguez; NBA players LeBron James and Dwayne Wade; professional golfers Tiger Woods and Michelle Wie; and professional tennis players Victoria Azarenka, Maria Sharapova, Venus and Serena Williams, Roger Federer, and Rafael Nadal. When Tiger Woods turned pro, Nike signed him to a five-year $100 million endorsement contract and made him the centerpiece of its campaign to make Nike a factor in the golf equipment and golf apparel marketplace. LeBron James's recent endorsement deal with Nike was said to be worth $120 million. Because soccer was such a popular sport globally, Nike had more endorsement contracts with soccer athletes than with athletes in any other sport; track and field athletes had the second-largest number of endorsement contracts.

EXHIBIT 6   Nike's Sales of Nike Brand Footwear, Apparel, and Equipment, by Geographic Region, Fiscal Years 2009–2011

Sales Revenues and Earnings (in millions)	Fiscal Years Ending May 31		
	2011	2010	2009
North America			
Revenues—Nike Brand footwear	$ 5,109	$ 4,610	$ 4,694
Nike Brand apparel	2,105	1,740	1,740
Nike Brand equipment	364	346	344
Total Nike Brand revenues	$ 7,578	$ 6.696	$ 6,778
Earnings before interest and taxes	$ 1,750	$ 1,538	$ 1,429
Profit margin	23.0%	23.0%	21.1%
Western Europe			
Revenues—Nike Brand footwear	$ 2,327	$ 2,320	$ 2,385
Nike Brand apparel	1,266	1,325	1,463
Nike Brand equipment	217	247	291
Total Nike Brand revenues	$ 3,810	$ 3,892	$ 4,139
Earnings before interest and taxes	$ 721	$ 856	$ 939
Profit margin	18.9%	22.0%	22.7%
Central & Eastern Europe			
Revenues—Nike Brand footwear	$ 600	$ 558	$ 673
Nike Brand apparel	356	354	468
Nike Brand equipment	75	81	106
Total Nike Brand revenues	$ 1,031	$ 993	$ 1,247
Earnings before interest and taxes	$ 233	$ 253	$ 394
Profit margin	22.6%	25.5%	31.6%
Greater China			
Revenues—Nike Brand footwear	$ 1,164	$ 953	$ 940
Nike Brand apparel	789	684	700
Nike Brand equipment	107	105	103
Total Nike Brand revenues	$ 2,060	$ 1,742	$ 1,743
Earnings before interest and taxes	$ 777	$ 637	$ 575
Profit margin	37.7%	36.6%	33.0%
Japan			
Revenues—Nike Brand footwear	$ 396	$ 433	$ 430
Nike Brand apparel	302	357	397
Nike Brand equipment	68	92	99
Total Nike Brand revenues	$ 766	$ 882	$ 926
Earnings before interest and taxes	$ 114	$ 180	$ 205
Profit margin	14.9%	20.4%	22.1%
Emerging Markets			
Revenues—Nike Brand footwear	$ 1,897	$ 1,458	$ 1,185
Nike Brand apparel	657	577	477
Nike Brand equipment	182	164	166

(Continued)

EXHIBIT 6   *(Continued)*

Sales Revenues and Earnings (in millions)	Fiscal Years Ending May 31		
	2011	2010	2009
Total Nike Brand revenues	$ 2,736	$ 2,199	$ 1,828
Earnings before interest and taxes	$ 688	$ 521	$ 364
Profit margin	25.1%	23.7%	19.9%
All Regions			
Revenues—Nike Brand footwear	$11,493	$10,332	$10,307
Nike Brand apparel	5,475	5,037	5,245
Nike Brand equipment	1,013	1,035	1,109
Total Nike Brand revenues	$17,981	$16,404	$16,661
Earnings before interest and taxes	$ 4,283	$ 3,985	$ 3,906
Profit margin	23.8%	24.3%	23.4%

Note 1: Nike Brand data does not include Nike Golf and other Nike-owned businesses such as Converse, Cole-Haan, and Hurley, all of which are separately organized and do not break their activities down by geographic region for reporting purposes. Nike Golf had revenues of $623 million in fiscal 2011, $638 million in fiscal 2010, and $648 million in fiscal 2009.

Note 2: The revenue and earnings figures for all geographic regions include the effects of currency exchange fluctuations.

Source: Nike's 10-K Report for Fiscal 2011, pp. 21–24.

Research and Development   Nike management believed R&D efforts had been and would continue to be a key factor in the company's success. Technical innovation in the design of footwear, apparel, and athletic equipment received ongoing emphasis in an effort to provide products that helped reduce injury, enhance athletic performance, and maximize comfort.

In addition to Nike's own staff of specialists in the areas of biomechanics, chemistry, exercise physiology, engineering, industrial design, and related fields, the company utilized research committees and advisory boards made up of athletes, coaches, trainers, equipment managers, orthopedists, podiatrists, and other experts who reviewed designs, materials, concepts for product improvements, and compliance with product safety regulations around the world. Employee athletes, athletes engaged under sports marketing contracts, and other athletes wear-tested and evaluated products during the design and development process.

Manufacturing   About 98 percent of Nike's footwear was produced by contract manufacturers in Vietnam, China, Indonesia, and India, but the company had manufacturing agreements with independent factories in Argentina, Brazil, India, and Mexico to manufacture footwear for sale primarily within those countries. Nike-branded apparel was manufactured outside of the United States by independent contract manufacturers located in 33 countries; most production occurred in China, Thailand, Vietnam, Malaysia, Sri Lanka, Indonesia, Turkey, Cambodia, El Salvador, and Mexico.

In 2011, Nike established a fiscal 2015 revenue target of $28–$30 billion and reaffirmed its ongoing target of annual earnings per share growth in the 14–16 percent range.

The adidas Group

The mission of The adidas Group is to be the global leader in the sporting goods industry with brands built on a passion for sports and a sporting lifestyle. Headquartered in Germany, its businesses and brands consist of:

- **adidas**—a designer and marketer of active sportswear, uniforms, footwear, and sports products in football, basketball, soccer, running, training, outdoor, and six other categories (74.0 percent of Group sales in 2011).

- **Reebok**—a well-known global provider of athletic footwear for multiple uses, sports and fitness apparel, and accessories (14.7 percent of Group sales in 2011).

- **TaylorMade-adidas Golf**—a designer and marketer of TaylorMade golf equipment, adidas golf shoes and golf apparel, and Ashworth golf apparel (7.8 percent of Group sales in 2011).

- **Rockport**—a designer and marketer of dress, casual, and outdoor footwear that largely targeted

EXHIBIT 7 Financial Highlights for The adidas Group, 2006–2011 (in millions of €)

Income Statement Data	2011	2010	2009	2008
Net sales	€13,334	€11,990	€10,381	€10,799
Gross profit	6,344	5,730	4,712	5,256
Gross profit margin	47.5%	47.8%	45.4%	48.7%
Operating profit	1,011	894	508	1,070
Operating profit margin	7.6%	7.5%	4.9%	9.9%
Net income	670	567	245	642
Net profit margin	5.0%	4.7%	2.4%	5.9%
Balance Sheet Data				
Inventories	€ 2,482	€ 2,119	€ 1,471	€ 1,995
Working capital	2,154	1,972	1,649	1,290
Net Sales by Brand				
adidas	€ 9,867	€ 8,714	€ 7,520	€ 7,821
Reebok	1,962	1,913	1,603	1,717
TaylorMade-adidas Golf	1,044	909	831	812
Rockport	261	252	232	243
Reebok-CCM Hockey	210	200	177	188
Net Sales by Product				
Footwear	€ 6,275	€ 5,389	€ 4,642	€ 4,919
Apparel	5,734	5,380	4,663	4,775
Equipment	1,335	1,221	1,076	1,105
Net Sales by Region				
Western Europe	€ 3,922	€ 3,543	€ 3,261	€ 3,527
European emerging markets	1,596	1,385	1,122	1,179
North America	3,102	2,805	2,362	2,520
Greater China	1,229	1,000	967	1,077
Other Asian markets	2,125	1,972	1,647	1,585
Latin America	1,368	1,285	1,006	893

Source: Company annual reports, 2011, 2010, and 2009.

metropolitan professional consumers (2.0 percent of Group sales in 2011).

- **Reebok CCM Hockey**—one of the world's largest designers, makers, and marketers of hockey equipment and apparel under the brand names Reebok Hockey and CCM Hockey (1.6 percent of Group sales in 2011).

In 2011, The adidas Group produced record sales of €13.3 billion, increased profits to €670 (from €567 million in 2010), and significantly reduced long-term borrowings from €1,337 million to €991 million. Exhibit 7 shows the company's financial highlights for 2008–2011.

The company sold products in virtually every country of the world. In 2011, its extensive product offerings were marketed through third-party retailers (sporting goods chains, department stores, independent sporting goods retailer buying groups, lifestyle retailing chains, and Internet retailers), 1,355 company-owned and franchised adidas and Reebok "concept" stores, 734 company-owned adidas and Reebok factory outlet stores, 312 other adidas and Reebok stores with varying formats, and various company websites (such as www.adidas.com, www.reebok.com, and www.taylormadegolf.com).

Like Under Armour and Nike, both adidas and Reebok were actively engaged in sponsoring major sporting events, teams, and leagues and in using athlete endorsements to promote their products. Recent high-profile sponsorships and promotional partnerships included Official Sportwear Partner of the 2012 Olympic Games (adidas), outfitting all volunteers, technical staff, and officials as well as all the athletes in Team Great Britain; Official Sponsors and ball supplier of the 2010 FIFA World Cup, the 2011 FIFA Women's World Cup Germany, and numerous other important soccer tournaments held by FIFA and the Union of European Football Associations or UEFA (adidas); Official Outfitters of NHL (Reebok), NFL (Reebok), NBA (adidas), WNBA (adidas), and NBA-Development League (adidas); Official Apparel and Footwear Outfitter for Boston Marathon (adidas); Official Licensee of Major League Baseball fan and lifestyle apparel (Reebok). Athletes that were under contract to endorse some of the company's brands included NBA players Derrick Rose, Tim Duncan, and John Wall; professional golfers Paula Creamer (LPGA), Jim Furyk, Sergio Garcia, Retief Goosen, Dustin Johnson, Kenny Perry, Justin Rose, and Mike Weir; soccer player David Beckham; and various participants in the 2012 Summer Olympics in London. In 2003, David Beckham, who had been wearing adidas products since the age of 12, signed a $160 million lifetime endorsement deal with adidas that called for an immediate payment of $80 million and subsequent payments said to be worth an average of $2 million annually for the next 40 years.[7] adidas was anxious to sign Beckham to a lifetime deal not only to prevent Nike from trying to sign him but also because soccer was considered the world's most lucrative sport and adidas management believed that Beckham's endorsement of adidas products resulted in more sales than all of the company's other athlete endorsements combined. In 2011, the company launched its biggest-ever global advertising campaign for adidas-brand products. Companywide expenditures for advertising, event sponsorships, athlete endorsements, and other marketing activities were €1.36 billion in 2011, up from €1.29 billion in 2010.

Research and development activities commanded considerable emphasis at The adidas Group. Management had long stressed the critical importance of innovation in improving the performance characteristics of its products. New apparel and footwear collections featuring new fabrics, colors, and the latest fashion were introduced on an ongoing basis to heighten consumer interest, as well as to provide performance enhancements—35 "major product launches" were conducted in 2009, 39 in 2010, and 48 in 2011. About 1,000 people were employed in R&D activities at 11 locations, of which 5 were devoted to adidas products, 3 to Reebok products, and 1 each for TaylorMade-adidas Golf, Rockport, and Reebok-CCM Hockey. In addition to its own internal activities, the company drew upon the services of well-regarded researchers at universities in Canada, England, and Germany. R&D expenditures in 2011 were €115 million, up from €81 million in 2008, €86 million in 2009, and €102 million in 2010.

Over 95 percent of production was outsourced to 308 independent contract manufacturers located in China and other Asian countries (77 percent), the Americas (15 percent), Europe (7 percent), and Africa (1 percent). The Group operated 9 relatively small production and assembly sites of its own in Germany (1), Sweden (1), Finland (1), the United States (4), Canada (3), and China (1). Close to 97 percent of the Group's production of footwear was performed in Asia; annual volume sourced from footwear suppliers had ranged from a low of 191 million pairs to a high of 245 million pairs during 2007–2011. During the same time frame, apparel production ranged from 239 million to 321 million units and the production of hardware products ranged from 34 million to 51 million units.

ENDNOTES

[1] Daniel Roberts, "Under Armour Gets Serious," *Fortune*, November 7, 2011, p. 153.
[2] Ibid., p. 156.
[3] Ibid.
[4] Ibid.

[5] As stated on p. 53 of Under Armour's Prospectus for its Initial Public Offering of common stock, dated November 17, 2005.
[6] Company 10-K reports, 2009, 2010, and 2011.

[7] Steve Seepersaud, "5 of the Biggest Athlete Endorsement Deals," posted at www.askmen.com, accessed February 5, 2012.